THE BURNING BUSH

John Drury was born in 1936 and studied at Trinity Hall and Westcott House, Cambridge. He served as a curate in London and as a college chaplain in Oxford and Cambridge before being appointed a canon of Norwich Cathedral in 1973. He then taught at the University of Sussex from 1979 until 1981 when he became Dean of King's College, Cambridge, responsible for the worship in its renowned chapel.

In his work as a New Testament scholar he emphasizes the importance of combining historical study of the gospels with an appreciation of their literary qualities. A respected writer, he is the author of *Tradition and Design in Luke's Gospel* (DLT) and *The Parables in the Gospels* (SPCK) and contributed to *The Literary Guide to the Bible* (Collins). An amateur painter and devotee of Mozart, he lives in Cambridge with his wife and two daughters.

THE ARCHBISHOP OF CANTERBURY'S
LENT BOOKS

JOHN DRURY

THE BURNING BUSH

With a Foreword by
the Archbishop of Canterbury

Collins
FOUNT PAPERBACKS
in association with Faith Press

First published in Great Britain by Fount Paperbacks, London
in 1990 in association with Faith Press

Copyright © John Drury 1990

Printed and bound in Great Britain by
William Collins Sons & Co. Ltd, Glasgow

For Clare, Jessica and Susannah

The author and publishers are grateful for permission to use material from T. S. Eliot, *Collected Poems 1909-1962* (Faber & Faber, 1963); *Selected Poetry of Rainer Maria Rilke* ed. and tr. S. Mitchell (Picador, 1981); and E. Muir, *Collected Poems 1921-1958* (Faber & Faber, 1960).

CONTENTS

FOREWORD

by the Archbishop of Canterbury

"To inherit a great religious tradition like Christianity", writes John Drury, requires "the open alertness of discovering it afresh".

Such "open alertness" is precisely what he helps us to achieve throughout this highly personal yet rarely idiosyncratic book. He does so in three ways. He makes us recognize the perennial interdependence of word, image, symbol and ritual within Christian culture. He shows us how the creative religious imagination can enhance Christian living, and he almost persuades us that the "post-orthodoxy" of our own times can strengthen rather than threaten our Christian identity. "Being free to choose", he tells us, "can be, possibly just is, more favourable to sincere and integrated Christianity than compulsion, although it gives us more to do."

Indeed it does. But this book — scholarly but never dull, accessible but never trite, and in style and content distinctively Drury's own — should help many Christians, and some non-Christians, in this important yet not impossible task.

Robert Cantuar

ACKNOWLEDGEMENTS:

And On Going Down and Out

... Only by the form, the pattern,
Can words or music reach
The stillness ...

T. S. ELIOT: "Burnt Norton"

Preachers say things which they forget, but a hearer may remember for a long time. Some thirty years ago, when Robert Runcie was Dean of Trinity Hall in Cambridge and I was a student there, he was preaching about the presence of Christ in the panelled intimacy of its little chapel. He closed his sermon by turning to the altar and quoting the three words from John 1:46 with which Jesus invited Nathanael to discipleship: "Come and see."

Why have I remembered that? First, I think, because it appealed to the basic business of an academic place, experiment. "Come and see" was a good text for people whose work consisted in making up their own minds about things by seeing how they worked out and what sense they made. It was apt to what we were about. But it was also strange. In an academic place you expect people to prefer theories. If they are religious they concern themselves with doctrines. And here was a teacher in earnest, pointing to an old piece of ritual furniture as the focus for our attention.

It was not as odd as all that. Robert Runcie was, and is,

11

an historian and pastor rather than a theoretician. Since that evening, historians at large have come to give a lot more attention to rituals. They have found that attention to the ceremonies of past societies, whether great national and civic ones or little domestic ones, has let them in to the innermost secrets of how they saw their world, how they arranged it, confirmed it and changed it. Historians used to be mainly concerned with the documents which top people left behind them. Now they are also interested in the rituals which brought them into public: what they wore, how they moved about the place; even what they ate, and how they ate it, at the feasts which were often important parts of such occasions. Other people than top people took part: the whole society of minor officials and clergy, merchants and beggars, housewives and children. And their humbler or private conventions, which ordered life at home and in the street, were also valuable clues to the quality of that whole life, rich in physical detail, which historians want to describe. Paintings are now as good historical evidence as treaties, table manners as coronations. How people moved and gesticulated can be even better evidence for what they thought and felt than what they said or wrote. And even in what they said and wrote, the manner of it, the lies and evasions and mistakes, can be as revelatory as what they got right. What is thought superficial can matter as much as what is counted profound.

There is religious value in all this. If the mighty have not been exactly put down from their seats by modern historians, they have been levelled by being integrated into the ordinariness of their societies and having the lowly foundations of their eminence disclosed. We know who made their seats, and how, and at what cost. And something very valuable about truth has been affirmed. It is that manner is a just judge. I may be saying something plausible or officially correct, but if I blush and fidget, or if my voice gets hesitant or shrill, I give away more truth than I would like. I may be saying something trite, or even making a quotation from the first chapter of the gospel of John but the relaxed and deliberate urgency of voice and posture make it truer than it would be otherwise. Manner matters. St Paul put it definitively in the thirteenth chapter of his first letter to the Corinthians: whatever we do is empty if it is not done in the way and manner of love. So literary critics who home in on the tone and structure of how something is written, are not abandoning their serious interest in truth. And religious people who go to church services are not less engaged with the truth of their religion than its theologians. Interest in what they do at church and how they do it, is as valid as interest in what they say there. When people going out of church thank the vicar for taking the service nicely, they are making a fundamental point.

The truth of the physical marks two great moments in modern fiction: which, incidentally, by its close attention to people's movements and other physical conventions is usually able to give us more truth and help than bare theory. The first moment comes from Proust's *Remembrance of Things Past*: a wonderfully delicate and elaborate act of recall, in which the moments of success and revelation have such physical triggers as the scent of may blossom or the sensation of stepping up onto the pavement backwards. The moment at which Proust tasted the little madeleine cake dipped in tea had the sacramental power of unleashing the whole truth of his childhood in a Norman town. The second moment comes from the poem of the Grand Inquisitor in Dostoyevsky's *The Brothers Karamazov*. It is the fictional invention of the intellectual Karamazov brother, Ivan, so it is naturally full of the intellectual energy of argument – all from the Grand Inquisitor himself and none from Christ who stands (thanks to fiction's magic with time) before him in unbroken silence. The kiss which Christ finally gives the Grand Inquisitor is an astonishing answer to the old man's closely reasoned indictment of him. Its phy- sicality short-circuits the argument of the man's monologue and makes the corners of his mouth twitch very slightly. What does it *say*? Very likely its rationale is the book's grand theme and theory that we are all responsible for one another, that we share the world by mutual acceptance if we are not to lose it by mutual murder. But it is better to keep away from theory and in with narrative actuality, and so see this gentle kiss as the counterpart of the betraying kiss of Judas in the gospels – which Dostoyevsky had assimilated in his prison camp.

Proust's cake and Dostoyevsky's kiss were both momentous points of transition. They changed everything, not least the apprehension of all that had gone before – which is, humanly speaking, just about everything. In religion there is nothing more important than transition: from darkness to light, from puberty to maturity, from isolation to community. This is because religion grasps the basic point that our lives are passings over and are ineluctably transient. Theory hovers around this, but true description and representation of it must come in forms that are as closely and clearly tied in to the passage of time as it is: narrative and ritual.

Here I come to my second acknowledgement. It is to an anthropologist whose study of myth and ritual, their structures and their functions, matured into clear insight into the shapes and workings of religion: Sir Edmund Leach.

Sadly, it has to be by way of memorial. I knew him in his last seven years when religion, and the Bible particularly, had become his chief study. I owe him a sense of the deep practicality and functional beauty of religion – doctrine and "all that stuff" as he called it, apart. He died while I was writing this book. But while he was ill I was able to tell him that what I had learned from him was formative of this Archbishop of Canterbury's Lent Book. A vividly and provocatively unorthodox man, he relished the apparent oddity of it. But as a matter of fact, Edmund Leach pointed me as firmly and creatively towards the crucial importance of ritual as Robert Runcie did. He was fascinated by rites of passage, the ceremonial crossings over from living to dead and dead to living, from the wild to the civilized and back again, from singleness to community, and so on. He was strongly aware of the numinous power which radiated from these thresholds. In the light of it he discovered the crucial importance of Jesus' movements in the gospels, particularly his frequent water-crossings on the way to mighty works of healing power and his withdrawals into solitude as preludes to community making. He was a critic of religion who was not only prompt to stigmatize its pretentiousness, but also happy to uncover the codes of the movements by which it helped people and brought them together.

Edmund Leach was a critic. As he looked, he thought and analysed. He acknowledged that, in the study of mankind, what the researcher observed out there in the field had to be matched with what went on inside his head. There had to be looking in as well as looking out for meaning to be born. This is a basic religious belief, the conviction that the microcosm matches the macrocosm: the movements and patterns of what goes on in the big world around us match the movements and patterns of what goes on in the little world inside us. The thinking never stops, so it had better be clear and good — above all, fitting or, in the old Prayer Book's words, *meet and right*.

This is important as we follow the movement of historians and anthropologists down into the physical world and out into its social web of ramifications. To go that way without thinking and analysing all the time as precisely as we can is dangerous folly. Totalitarian posters with their muscular bodies and gleaming machines, the base mysticism of blood and soil, and all the rubbish of pornography, gluttony and greed, mark the cruel waste which results from an irrational descent to matter. We lose our freedom and are driven, possessed. Rituals to justify such horror are promptly invented; the torch light parades and the raucous salutes. We must keep thinking, never surrendering the freedom and clarity which we have painfully got to in our heads to the excitement that is going on around. If we can do this at all, we will have achieved more than a negative job of hygiene. It will be fertile. Thinking carried down into the world of matter, out into the environing and social world, gets truth and searching power which it would not have got if it had stayed in the top of the head, making theories. This thought informs a poem of Rilke about one of those ancient sculpted torsos, bodies which have lost their heads, which we see in museums. It has not lost its head in the usual meaning of that phrase. Rather, thought has become more strongly present by suffusing the body.

We cannot know his legendary head
with eyes like ripening fruit. And yet his torso

is still suffused with brilliance from inside,
like a lamp, in which his gaze, now turned to low,

gleams in all its power. Otherwise
the curved breast could not dazzle you so, nor could
a smile run through the placid hips and thighs
to the dark centre where procreation flared.

Otherwise this stone would seem defaced
beneath the translucent cascade of the shoulders
and would not glisten like a wild beast's fur;

would not, from all the borders of itself,
burst like a star: for here there is no place
that does not see you. You must change your life.

R. M. RILKE: "Archaic Torso of Apollo"

Long ago Christians took over the attributes of Apollo, this Greek God of light and order, for their light-bringer, Christ. The fitness of doing that is confirmed in a modern setting by this poem. "We cannot know his legendary head ..." Attempts to find and isolate exactly what Christ thought about something run into the fact that, because he taught by word of mouth, what he said is only available to us in the versions of the other people who assimilated his teaching. It is there, but present in a body of people from whom he is inseparable: whether St Paul and the gospel writers or contemporaries of ours. That his presence has the power of a demand on us to change our lives, is precisely because it is so embodied. The eucharist, Christ's body present in its power to change other bodies by nourishing them, is its symbolic representation and the clue to how his presence comes and goes. We will be coming back there again and again to learn, like a pianist doing her five-finger exercises, the basic moves of living.

I have acknowledged my debt to these two people at length because it was a way of introducing this book's leading themes. But whenever I have felt that I was getting anywhere in my attempts to understand the wonderful things that I was writing about, I have also sensed vividly how much I owe to many other people and how really my life has, at its best, been participation in theirs. I cannot name them all. They include colleagues in college and chapel here at King's, the President of the Royal Academy who asked me to preach and so made me think about truth in pictures, my teachers and pupils, a lot of clergy and a few theologians. But most obviously, to think about life in terms of participation and development is to realize how deeply one's family matters. My parents got me going in all sorts of ways which carry on. I have been unusually lucky in the matter of aunts. And as for my wife and daughters, if there is anything here that may cheer them up one day, it will be a small return for the rich fare of kindness and good sense which they have lavished on me.

1

Symbols and Time

In church one Sunday, a poet was distracted. In the pew in front of him there was a woman, as devout as she was well-dressed. A louse appeared in the lace of her bonnet, then burrowed through it to appear, finally and publicly, at the top of her head: at which juncture other people noticed, winked and pointed. But the lady herself had no idea of what was going on. The last verse of the poem Burns wrote about the louse's journey is famous:

> O wad some Pow'r the giftie gie us
> *To see oursels as others see us!*
> It wad frae monie a blunder free us
>   An' foolish notion:
> What airs in dress an' gait wad lea'e us,
>   And ev'n Devotion!

Sharp observation of a little incongruity brought about that sharp moral. It cuts into the way we get ourselves up and go about, our "airs in dress an' gait". We don't realize that other people don't see them as we do. It even cuts into our religion or "Devotion", to which the same applies. We are so strongly armed with oblivious complacency that to penetrate it would require the intervention of "some Pow'r" from outside us. And the resulting change would be a "giftie". Burns knew very well that his homely language was here edging into the solemn speeches of theology about the gracious gifts of God. And he relished the way this let him probe a diseased and inflamed religious nerve.

Divine gifts sound nice and easy, but as often as not they are hard to take. They occur as shocks, minor or major. Often the minor ones are harder to take than the major, which at least have the high drama of catastrophe. For us to "see oursels as others see us" is always a jolting experience, and more usually comic than tragic. We even hide some of our virtues from ourselves; whether because they are a sort of second nature to us, or because our efforts to practise them come from an ashamed sense that we do not have them, or simply because they are not the virtues we would choose for our self-image. We hide our vices from ourselves for more obvious reasons of self-regard. So to be presented with them puts us at a loss – precisely, the loss of the image of ourselves to which we have got accustomed. Are we really like that? They say so, but it takes some effort to digest it. Even if we can see jokes which are on us, we do not often think them particularly funny.

As for individuals, so for groups. In the modern world, Christianity can be seen as others see it by its own adherents. This is because it has lost its Western monopoly as a way of picturing the world and can be sized up from the vantage points of other world-views: from secular science, psychology or history, or from the point of view of one of the other religions with which it shares the market as an available option. Faced by options we have to be critics, analysing as shrewdly and quickly as possible the value, use and pleasure of the competing possibilities.

For the past three hundred years, Christianity has been the subject of thorough and pervasive critiques. Its history has been assessed, not on its own terms as God's favourite and most energetically promoted concern, but as something that can be quite satisfactorily understood in quite different ways: as a means of coping with fundamental psychic forces in people, or as the product and the control of social and economic factors for which it is not entirely responsible. Its rituals can be appreciated by using the sort of dispassionate sympathy, the disinterested curiosity, which anthropologists bring to the study of societies which are not their own. Most dramatically, its sacred text, the Bible, has been minutely examined by the use of historical and literary analysis which is used on history and literature at large. A vast resource of biblical criticism has resulted.

Christians have not stood aside from this. Most of the greatest church historians and biblical critics have been devout believers, even clergy. They treated fellow-workers who were neither of these things as equals. If they disagreed with them, they presented their disagreements according to the rules of the republic of letters. Above that, they were moved by faith that it is fair and good for Christianity to see itself as others see it. If this was a gift of divine grace, their work was part of it. It was good because, like all religions and ideologies, Christianity is always on the verge of oblivious complacency and turning nasty. Critical thinking is the medicine against that. The Bible which they studied is, after all, as full of excoriating criticism of received or orthodox religion as it is of support for it. And their work was good in another way. Criticism brings out strengths and beauties in Christianity of which its adherents have become forgetful. Often the two go together. The critical clearing away of what is tawdry will make room and light for what is good and true.

If individual Christians have been energetic in the criticism of their own religion, the same cannot be said of the higher institutional levels of the churches. This is not surprising. Big aggregations of people are heavy and cumbersome. They are hard to get started. Once started they build up a momentum which makes them hard to stop or turn. In the biblical story it took an angel to stop the prophet Balaam on his inappropriate mission of denunciation, and even then his donkey saw it rather than himself. Bishops have to take whole dioceses with them and stay in company of some sort with their episcopal colleagues. Deans and vicars, not to mention journalists and scholars, travel lighter. As a result, the rest of us are confronted by contradictory invitations: to change and be nippy, or to be steady and loyal. How are we to decide?

Strategy and timing can be a consideration. As with the political electorate, there may be some rough sense in feeling that at a particular moment either change or tradition has had more than enough of a run on its own and it is time for its opposite. So the pendulum swings. But that sort of thing does not draw on our best capacities to think and feel. It is a reaction, not a free and deliberate choice. The weak human input is rewarded by weak results. God is not mocked. As we sow, so we reap, and the irresponsibility of mere reaction cannot expect much in response.

We could do better than these negative and slightly resentful reactions. We could get thinking, although it is hard and lonely work. We could refine our sensitivities by prayer for the grace of proper self-awareness. We could look for the changes which would freshen what is most valuable in tradition. And we could draw on the traditions which teach us how to change for the better rather than the worse. All this is more difficult and more interesting than reaction. This book will attempt it.

Symbols and Time

In particular, it will use two big features of the criticism of religion, both of them hot to handle, as ways of noticing the creativity in Christianity. The first is the conviction that religion is thoroughly symbolic. It is unwelcome to those who want religion to be based in the authority of unassailable fact alone. The second is that religion is thoroughly historical. It is suspect to those who want it to be changeless.

Symbols are not things apart. If anything, they are things between. As we know in our dreams, anything can be a symbol. Someone can be terrified or delighted by dreaming about a bird or an armchair. Whatever it was, they know that it stands between themselves and something else. To find out what that might be, and so why they felt as they did, they need to find out how this particular symbol radiates this particular feeling. How did the two get associated in the first place? Emphatically, symbols are not things apart from time. So some sort of criticism is required, and it is bound to be in some way historical: the unravelling of the symbol's story which is tied into someone's biography. Autobiography, in fact, is the name of this tricky game: the searching form of narrative self-criticism which was invented by the Christian theologian Augustine. Symbols are the visible tips of huge icebergs of the developed and developing associations which make up our selves. To come upon them is never to reach a dead end. More precisely, when we come upon a symbol we can stop dead or tiptoe round it, but if we do so we fail to open a door or cross a ford which was ours to go through. We have missed a chance of the sort of knowledge out of which wisdom is made. For a symbol is a point of entry into the whole network and story of persons and things which have crystallized it. It does not so much solve a problem as open up a whole field or city of meanings within which the problem can make sense as an inhabitant. This makes it very like a ritual. And we do best to treat it accordingly: not rushing to believe or disbelieve it, assent or deny, but rather playing with it, turning it over and around and letting it catch different lights, sleeping on it.

This sort of approach is much more promising for the Christian eucharist than head-on affirmation or denial of doctrines about it like transubstantiation. They need to be postponed. Later, they may prove very useful, and in chapter six we will in fact discuss the doctrine of transubstantiation. But first we have to make the very Protestant move of recognizing symbols as symbols, distinct from the world of actualities on which they draw and to which they give significant shape. Then we have to eat and drink the symbol. Physical as this is, it is still a part of the process of thinking. We are told to "take and eat this in remembrance ... in faith with thanksgiving": all activities of the mind and heart, which are indispensable. This is thinking in its mode of digestion and interiorizing, following upon thinking in the mode of sizing up what is before us. It is followed by a richer kind of sizing up, now including the experience of participation and of the symbol's linking on, through us who have assimilated it, to whatever we have to tackle in the world at large.

Behind the eucharist lies the process by which a man, Jesus, became symbolic and so lives on after his departure. It followed the same pattern: sizing up, assimilating, linking on. The Jesus of the gospels had a sharp eye for the symbolic behaviour in the world around him: the phylacteries and table manners of the devout, the use of the sacred law and of the temple. He knew what was in front of him and could distinguish the bogus from the true, the merely symbolic from the symbolically creative. But this critical faculty was not a block but a filter. Through it he drew deeply and widely on his whole environment. By bringing so much of it into himself and assimilating it by means of quite practical critical analysis, he became a point of entry into life for other people. His individual life and body became common bread by means of the process of digestion, not by mere gestures of approval or disapproval. And he survives by being eaten, interiorized into other lives. Church services are all in aid of this process. Jesus Christ is alive today symbolically, his life and death sustaining ours by giving them a meaning which other people can see and assimilate. When I said "the Jesus of the gospels" at the beginning of this paragraph it was because we only have Jesus in literary record as he is assimilated into those books, their words and shapes. The Jesus of the gospels has already moved from life to life, in a process of transmission and transformation which we cannot undo or reverse, but can study.

Thinking about symbols has already, and for a good while, taken us into the second feature of religion which must be examined: it is historical. This is part of its creativity. Symbols live or die within the stream of time. If they are not grasped and digested at moments in time by people living in time, they languish. If they are grasped, broken down and digested, something extraordinary but very common happens. They both change and become vividly themselves. They are like Moses' God-revealing burning bush, a consumed yet sustained presence. Just how this happens is a question with which this book is preoccupied, looking for help in the processes of artistic creation, ritual and critical study.

Among the first generations of Christians it occurred

with astonishing speed and fertility. The individual figure of Jesus became a community of versions of him, as one person after another interiorized him as their sustaining symbol. He lived, as symbols do, by association. The New Testament is only the relatively small surviving collection of all the versions they made, a tiny relic of their creativity. The story of his life itself became, not a single book authoritatively sealed off, but a family of four books which have fed off one another and provoked one another. Many other versions were forgotten or banned. He had been, and given, more than a single book or a single life could hold. So John's gospel, probably the youngest of this family, ends not with a definitive closure (you get that, incidentally, at the end of *Revelation*, a book desperately impatient to get to the end of history and the triumph of symbols over it), but with a wry reflection on the inadequacy of what has been written, when there was so much more that could have been written.

> And there are also many other things which Jesus did, the which, if they should be written every one, I suppose that even the world itself could not contain the books that should be written. (John 21:25)

It amounts to a confession, at the end of the most dogmatically confident and symbolically brilliant of the gospels, that it is after all only a selection — and so, a version. The evangelist's self-awareness is liberating for his readers. Now it is over to them, who have read and inwardly digested his version, to think and live their own.

"Over to them." The symbols let this historical transition happen. Their place is the ford, the threshold, the crossroads. They enable crossing-over. But with all the movement and fertility which they germinate, is there any order? The exuberant creativity is obvious enough. It is like a June hedgerow bursting with all kinds of flourishings. But where is the control? It is not identifiable or isolable as an external authority over and above it all. It is in among it all and within each organism. It is among it in the way the growth of any one plant or animal controls the growth of any other, checking it, feeding it and feeding off it — there is social control. Then going further in and penetrating as far as we can go into individual plants and animals we find that each of these organisms is inwardly structured by minute codes, molecular chains which make up messages of growth and determine growth. It is extremely difficult to isolate and identify these codes, but we will try. If we have any success at all, it will be a great gain in the self-awareness which could change our "airs in dress an' gait ... And ev'n Devotion". For we will have learned something about the inner lives which determine our social reactions and contributions, and something about the social interactions by which we live off and for one another. We need to know about them because they are well able to lead to disaster, to make individual or collective chaos in the human world and the natural world which humans now control. So any knowledge that we can get will have the character of the saving knowledge which is called wisdom because it has learned to distinguish between what we can control and what we cannot. It is the critical faculty at its most useful and serene.

2

The Embarrassment of Riches

To be a Christian nowadays is to inherit a vast estate.
Christianity is nearly two thousand years old. Even that is
a minimal time span to put on it. St John believed that its
essence, the divine Word incarnated in Jesus, predated
creation. A more empirical view of its history would have
to take account of the fact that in its first three centuries,
before it became the orthodox religion of the whole
Mediterranean world, it assimilated a thousand years of
Jewish tradition — itself nourished by the ancient cultures
of Egypt and Mesopotamia — and more than five hundred
years of Greek life. Although it was a new religion, or
because it was, it understood itself as the heir and fulfilment
of all this. Although it focused on the single and individual
figure of Jesus, it understood him as the culmination of it
all: the Christ, the divine Word. Christian orthodoxy, when
it came, was as much of a massive inclusion of all sorts of
diverse stuff as a sharp and single thing. It was put in creeds
which every Christian recited and appropriated at his
baptismal initiation. They were short. It took only a minute
or two to say them. Yet they covered the whole of time
from creation to "the life of the world to come". This vast
sweep was integrated round the turning point of Jesus.

Christianity, this staggering achievement, is now no
longer a universal orthodoxy. It has split into hundreds of
churches and versions. And it, or rather they, live alongside
other faiths, some of them comparably venerable and rich

and rival claimants to be the universal religion of human beings.

Nor is it any longer in sole charge of its own inheritance. Its literature is open to the analytical inspection of any critic who wants to try out on it the skills he has worked out elsewhere. This is simply because it is available as literature. Its doctrines are open to the more or less sympathetic probings of philosophers who owe it no allegiance, its history to historians already in business. Its wonderful artistic achievements are accessible in concert halls and on discs, in museums and picture books and television programmes, on the itineraries of package holidays. You do not have to participate in liturgy to get them. And even if you do decide that that is the best place to appreciate them because it is their native context, you will not be held up for a check on your baptismal credentials at the doors of King's College Chapel, St Peter's Rome, or the Church of the Holy Sepulchre in Jerusalem.

A hundred years or so ago, it was plausible to prophesy that Christianity would succumb to criticism, disappear from the face of the earth, and be superseded by science or socialism. It has not, and does not look as if it will. Indeed at present the most intransigent and reactionary versions of it do brisk business. They look over their shoulders in annoyance and disdain at the liberal and progressive versions which have not faded away either. The liberal Christians were wrong to think that reactionary Christians would be extinguished by the relativisms of modern society. They have, instead, found themselves a place within it as a protest group so strong and organized as to bid for power and sometimes achieve it. But these same reactionary Christians are wrong to think that the liberals are hopelessly outdated relics. The liberal virtues of generosity and flexibility are as indispensable as ever.

So the contemporary Christian is faced with a highly paradoxical state of affairs in his religion. It has lost nothing. On the contrary, it is now possible on a much bigger scale than it ever was before, to recover and feed on forms of Christianity which have been superseded. The gnostic Christians of the first centuries or of medieval Languedoc, persecuted then as heretics by the orthodox, can now appeal to us by their unworldly individualism and their fine sense of the inappropriateness of structures of worldly power to the religion of Jesus. We can compare them with the orthodox bishops and kings who eliminated them in the name of the collective church with power and responsibility in the world. The comparison will not be conclusively to their disadvantage. They may even show up better than their orthodox victors. Until very recently church music meant recent church music. The work of Josquin or Monteverdi had its day and was then discarded. Now, modern composers have difficulty in getting themselves a niche alongside their forebears from the fourteenth through to the nineteenth century. When we remember the extraordinary power of music to arouse and shape the emotions and atmosphere which are so fundamental to religion, we realize that this is no side-issue. The inmost piety of a Protestant can now owe a lot to the great resource of Catholic music, and be all the better for it. Even the services themselves are now a matter of choice in the Church of England: old-fashioned Prayer Book, the latest style with "you" instead of "thou", or something in between.

Yet something has been lost, and it is major. While all the bits and pieces which make up Christianity are more, and not less, available to us, the centralizing powers which held it all together have lost control. For Protestants, this was the Bible. The Bible is still there to comfort, teach and inspire – and that in a host of new translations. But it is optional, not compulsory, reading. A certain unconscious optionality has, in fact, been exercised on it all the time by those, including the architects and upholders of orthodoxy, who ignored some of its major features and made much of minor ones. It could not have been otherwise. The Bible is far too big and diverse to be inserted into any scheme. Job and Ecclesiastes will stick out if nothing else does. But now we know about this. Unconscious selection has become conscious. We can notice ourselves doing it, criticize ourselves for doing it, and those who do not notice for not noticing. In Roman Catholicism the centralizing authority was the papacy. The Pope is still there and more visible than ever before. Television and Pope-mobiles make his dignified good looks familiar. He has the worldwide audience which his office has always claimed in a way beyond the wildest dreams of most of his predecessors. But his power of absolute command has diminished so dramatically that even in a reactionary phase it cannot be totally reclaimed. Liberation, and liberal, theologians are papally rebuked – then carry on with what they were doing before. They need not expect ecclesiastical preferment, but the publishers will not be any the less eager to give them contracts and they will have more time for the writing which annoyed the Pope in the first place. His difficulties are not only with intellectuals. His unambiguous ban on effective birth control peters out among ordinary people who make up their own minds about it and remain Catholics. The Queen, as Supreme Governor of the Church of England, has no power to direct the affairs of the Church under her theoretical control, even if she wanted such an appalling task. She makes Christmas broadcasts which appeal persuasively to her subjects' better natures and are reinforced by her personal example.

So if we go to the top we are faced, after all, with the fundamental ingredient of Christianity, the individual person. Christians exist as individuals. A Christian may be the only person in the family to be one, and may or may not want to coerce the other members of it into the same allegiance. Enormous resources are available to him or her. But he or she has to choose from them, intuitively or deliberately, and is supported and fed (rather than coerced) by the common life of the particular church which he or she has chosen (again!) to go to – not necessarily the parish church.

How are we to make sense of all this? We started this chapter by getting a rough sense of where we are in Christian history. We inherit all that was worked out in the centuries when Christianity was the orthodox ideology of Europe. But we do so in a world where it is no longer either obligatory or exclusive. Both externally and internally, socially and individually, we are post-orthodox. Even if our practice and thinking are as orthodox as we can make them, that is still the version we prefer, a matter of choice rather than imposition. Two positive things follow from this. The first is historical, the second to do with the positive quality of optionality itself.

The historical consequence of our situation concerns the practical question of the use of past history in order to understand our present needs: where shall we look in Christian history for sympathetic company? Living in a time of post-orthodox Christianity means that we can find a lot in common with the pre-orthodox Christianity of the three centuries *before* it became the unified religion of the Roman

Empire. We are more like the churches and the Christians of the New Testament. In view of the religious creativity and vivacity of the New Testament, let alone its traditionally normative authority, this is a very substantial compensation for what we have lost. The New Testament is pre-orthodox in a very precise and spectacular way. There is, as we have already noticed, not one gospel but four. One would suit orthodox uniformity better, and Christians did indeed homogenize them as best they could into single versions called harmonies. But note the plural! No harmony could dominate because each was based, however unconsciously, on selection. It could never be *the* version because it was so obviously only *a* version. And the four remained, secure in the official canon which none of the harmonies got into. They had more than that security. They had lives of their own. They had their individualities, barely noticed through the orthodox centuries which were not ready for them. But now we are ready, and can feel something like the excitement of the first Christians discovering in *their* sacred scriptures meanings long latent. We notice the difference of Mark's Jesus, fierce and mysterious, from the gentle and transparently lucid teacher of Luke. We can sympathize with Matthew's efforts to put a touch of the brake on the headlong assault on tradition in Mark's pages by insisting that Jesus also fulfilled and continued tradition. When we turn to Paul's letters, we find an individual, utterly convinced of the God-given and universal truth of his message, who yet had no authority, other than the power and weakness of his own pleading, to get it across to other people or to warn them off different versions, some of them recommended by apostles with more obvious authority than himself, the radical latecomer. Like a Christian today, even a Christian leader today, he could only plead and wait hopefully for their (optional) commitment.

The second feature of our post-orthodox state which matches pre-orthodox Christianity is this optionality itself. Being free to choose can be, possibly just is, more favourable to sincere and integrated Christianity than compulsion, though it gives us more to do. What we choose is so much more our own, personal to us as the clothes we choose to wear and the food we choose to eat. So it more readily becomes the sort of second nature to us which is what religion ought to be to work properly and convince people.

But how should we choose when there is so bewilderingly much to choose from? It is some comfort, useful in steadying us and quietening panic, to know that we have company. The Christians of the New Testament lived in a similar world. It was peopled with gurus and prophets, official and unofficial holy men, priests, wandering counsellors and divinized rulers. There were shrines and temples, sacred woods and rivers, holy books, rites and mysteries. Even within their new religion there was choice, a Corinthian Christian convert havering between the gospel as propounded by Paul or by Peter or by Apollos (1 Corinthians 1:12), tempted into partisanship and without New Testament or Pope to decide for him. They were on their own.

But not entirely. Religions, like people in general, have parents. Following parental leads or contradicting them helps them find their way. People develop by first drinking in what their parents give, then adapting it by questioning it. They take and they criticize, parental faults being as useful in mapping out their own courses as parental virtues. Christianity's parent is Judaism. While Christianity still lacked its own holy scripture, it had the parental library of the Old Testament. Its relation to it is ideally put at the end of the second chapter of Luke's gospel. Religious and natural parent-child relations are combined there. Jesus was twelve, the critical age of crossing-over from childhood to adulthood, from dependence to responsibility. Aptly to his age, he is first with his parents on Passover pilgrimage to Jerusalem and then obliviously absent from them. What took him away from them was his own, independent interest in his inherited religious tradition. He had to take it upon himself. When his parents noticed his absence and went back to look for him, they found him "sitting in the midst of the doctors [of the law, the tradition of which they were guardians and interpreters of] both hearing them and asking them questions". That receptive and critical attitude was, and is, the ideal Christian relation to scriptural tradition. Jesus called it "being about my Father's business" when his parents took him to task for it. A more exact, but less elegant, translation of the Greek would be "occupied in the things of my Father".

What does the phrase mean? An obvious answer is that the "things" or "business" of God the Father were, very precisely, the venerable scriptures which the twelve-year-old and his seniors were debating. But that collapses everything into a thing, a text, and leaves out the people concerned, which ignores a large part of what the story is about, its characters. And since the story is exemplary, it would encourage the idea that any sort of Bible reading would do so long as it was *Bible* reading and regardless of quality, because it would automatically be an involvement in God's business. If we take the whole story as the meaning-making setting of the phrase, we get a richer answer which includes, instead of ignoring, the quality of reading. Deliberately, the story presents Jesus at that betwixt-and-between age of twelve. He is an individual in the flow of time, crossing over from his past to his future, on a threshold between states. His attitude towards the tradition which occupies him matches the fore-and-aft character of its narrative moment by also facing two ways. He hears what tradition has to say. And he questions it. The quality of his preoccupation consists in this double response by a person moving through a stage in life. "Being about my Father's business" includes it all: hallowed tradition heard and questioned by an individual on the move and at a particular transitional moment.

This is an exemplary story, a paradigm of the use of tradition. It mixes confidence and modesty. Jesus had no doubt as to what he was about: God, no less. The early Christians shared that sureness. But it is a dangerous thing, and it matters very much how it is believed and used. Both sides in the disaster of the First World War believed it of themselves and we all have depressing experience of headlong possessors of it. The manner of it is crucial. Luke knew that its narrative, temporal nature was integral to its quality. This was what Jesus did then. It was continuous with everything that he did before and after, but it was not repeated. Other occasions required other probings of other scriptures; or foursquare affirmations of texts previously questioned. It did not end his engagement with the texts or foreclose other people doing so. It was right for then. So we still pick and choose from the wealth of tradition, listening to it so that we can say something true for now, for this passing moment. Its aptness to that moment will always be part of its quality. Obedience to time is the humbling corrective of over-confidence.

But it can be disabling on its own. Obsession with the

moment and whether we are handling it right makes us look at our own steps, lose our sense of direction and stumble. Then, like a tightrope walker, we need to look beyond, at what we have not yet got, in order to stay upright and on course. God is very decidedly beyond us, an aim rather than a secure possession. God is the quality which we have not yet caught but which appeals to our inmost hearts and minds as meant for us: our own and not our own. Being about the divine business is tantamount to being preoccupied with, for example, the goodness which we glimpse in the text and try to match with the good interpretation which we can only make if we refuse the temptation to cut a heretical or orthodox figure, be clever or holy. The widest range and the most self-forgetful concentration must go together. So Paul took his leave of the Philippians.

> Finally, brethren, whatsoever things are true, whatsoever things are honest, whatsoever things are just, whatsoever things are pure, whatsoever things are lovely, whatsoever things are of good report; if there be any virtue, and if there be any praise, think on these things. Those things, which ye have both learned, and received, and heard, and seen in me, do: and the God of peace shall be with you. (Philippians 4:8-9)

3

Food for Tradition

"Finally, brethren ..." In spite of its ostensible function as a goodbye, a closing down of business, the quotation from Philippians which ended the previous chapter works at a lower level as a starter. The writer takes his leave by setting his readers to the infinite task of thinking about anything and everything of value. In fact, all leave-takings are like that: moments in time when the pastness of the past is made so inescapable that we feel our temporality sharply, including the future. We press advice, kisses, sandwiches or a good book on those who are leaving us. Questions of quality and value become crucial as the only bridge between what has gone and what is to come. They give the numinous quality which glows on every threshold. Such moments are intense, condensed bottlenecks in the temporal flow of our lives.

Looking at the quotation from Philippians again, it shows itself to be more of an unconcluded narrative than a full stop. A net was cast wide to catch everything good; the honest, the just, the pure, the lovely. Then, as if the thing for the reader to look at changed from the net to the fisherman hauling it in, the departing writer called attention to himself, the Paul who had collected all this into himself and so made it available to other people. What he had embodied as an individual person was now to be assimilated by the reader as his task for the present and the future. It pointed to that future with its promise "the God of peace shall be with you".

Just as we thought we had stopped we are off again, but far from aimlessly. We have been shown how and where to go: first a gathering of multifarious good things; then an appropriation of them into the individual system by thought; then the injunction to get on with working them out in action towards the promise of peace. Things move. We move. Goodness and truth have a story. They are historical.

This is not news to Christians. Their central doctrine of the incarnation of divine goodness in Jesus' biography proclaims it. But it is another of those gifts of God that are hard to take. The temporality of ourselves is something we find difficult to grasp in serious detail. Saints have tried to get it into their heads by contemplating skulls and graves. Religion is just as reluctant to get to grips with it. It thinks that its thoughts and doctrines are time-proof. Certainly they can last much longer than the human bodies which thought them up, adapted or dismantled them. They can carry quality and value from the departed to the survivors. But they only do so in the flow of time and do not escape from it. They too have their stories. Thoughts and doctrines are, with a little expertise, as dateable as costumes, chairs or music.

We will now look at two Christian doctrines with the aim of understanding something about the process of collecting and selecting, assimilating and explaining which was involved in their making. They are corporate instances of the business of choosing which confronts us individually. The first is the doctrine of incarnation itself, which is so central to how Christians think and feel. It takes us into the pre-orthodox world of New Testament Christianity. The second belongs to our own time, is still in dispute and may or may not get settled and accepted. It is the doctrine of the priesthood of women.

When the first Christians made their thinking out of the tradition available to them, the dominant written part of that tradition was Old Testament scripture. They constantly referred to it because it was their prime authority. The idea that God could become incarnate in a human being was not there. Instead, there was a wealth of other ideas about how God related to people by human means. He inspired prophets with his messages or sent angels to deliver them. Wise men and good rulers could aptly be called God's sons. The same title was given to angels and to the Jewish nation at large. There was another, strange, title, "Son of Man". The prophet Ezekiel used it of himself in a deprecating manner to show up the transient lowliness of his humanity in the face of his divine vocation. In the Book of Daniel it had an opposite meaning, referring to a super-powered human being still to come as God's ultimate agent at the end of the world. The undecided ambiguity of this title made it apt to the humiliated yet triumphant figure of Jesus, and it is dramatically deployed in the gospels. And there was the Messiah or Christ, originally an anointed king like David, but in the later centuries preceding Christianity transferred to the realm of future hope for a divinely appointed ruler-to-come. So there was a lot, and there was a marked tendency to project its definition or revelation into the future, leaving it open-ended in the present, waiting for its definition. But there was not yet divine incarnation, though when it did eventually come it was to be the arch-definition for Christians.

This plural, fertile and future-turned state of affairs carried over into the earlier New Testament gospels, where Jesus had a variety of traditional titles. For Mark and Matthew he was Messiah/Christ, Son of Man and Son of God. He was the fulfilment of the many hopes which glowed like live embers in the old writings and now flared into vivid and consuming life. Matthew rejoiced both in the continuity and the newness of it when he made his frequent announcements that something in his story of Jesus fulfilled a scriptural prophecy. For Luke, Jesus was himself a prophet, the ultimate prophet warning the nation of approaching doom: Elijah returned to raise the dead, recall the nation to obedience to God and ascend into heaven.

Jewish scriptural tradition provided, apparently, more than enough for the evangelists' work of presenting Jesus to the world as revelation of God. Old visions and titles sprang to him like filings to a magnet, finding at last a single human centre. A large part of the secret of the prodigious energy of early Christianity lies in the fact that so many scattered lights and forces were concentrated into the tale of a single man. With hindsight we can say that this condensation brought these evangelists to the edge of thinking of Jesus as incarnate divinity. But they did not do it, finding enough work to do in their reforging of the rich tradition which itself stopped short of incarnation.

But another, neighbouring, popular tradition had it. Greek religion was full of tales of gods coming to earth in human form, going a-begging or courting. Alexander the Great believed himself to be such an epiphany – and he was the man who set Greek culture on its course of expansion into Palestine and beyond, making it the neighbour of Judaism and ultimately causing the Christian New Testament to be written in Greek. His successors, and the Roman emperors, repeated the claim to intimate relation with divinity, even sonship. It was taken up by lesser fry, more or less plausibly. So it was as Christianity settled into the wider Greek world, feeding on some of its ways of thinking and picturing the relations of humanity and divinity, that the possibility of incarnation becoming the cornerstone of Christology was opened to it. It was a powerful idea, got by crossing over from the parent tradition to the "heathen" world — a coming-of-age present, perhaps. It would never have come about if the Christians had only been stay-at-home guardians of stable tradition.

The key figure is John, the fourth evangelist. It is in his gospel that the incarnation of the divine Word in Jesus first appears as explicit Christian doctrine, wonderfully articulated in myth, story and discourse. It is worth pausing at this great moment, some of its power familiar from the reading of John 1 as the gospel on Christmas Day, and recapitulate. How did it come about? We have found two factors. The first has the character of continuity. The previous evangelists had focused all that they could find in Jewish scripture about God's intimacy with people onto Jesus. It remained only to find a single idea, deep and strong and unified enough to include it all and pinpoint the centre itself. Incarnation was it. The second factor had the character of discontinuity. It was in the process of Christianity's breaking from its Jewish parent, absorbing a religious tradition alien to it, that it was able to think something so illuminating that the light from it flooded back over all previous story and thought, making manifest previously hidden hints and implications. The move disclosed the truth. It also, incidentally, left disfiguring traces of anti-Semitism on John's great achievement in the form of frequent damning references to "the Jews" as Jesus' enemies — although he was one himself. Masterpieces, Christian ones not excluded, have their seamy sides.

But there is something in this whole development which

is worth thinking about in the relation of history to the revelation of truth. It is as ordinary as it is important. Something happens. There and then, thinking on our feet, we interpret what it means. But it does not stop there. If it was something that mattered, we go on wondering about it and may discover later that our initial interpretation was faulty. Then we have to reconsider everything that has occurred in between. Early in Proust's vast novel *Remembrance of Things Past*, the narrator is an adolescent on a country walk with his parents. He lags behind and, through the flowering hawthorns which hide a rich estate, sees a girl who attracts him. She makes a sudden gesture. Shy and insecure, he thinks it means that she is irritated by his attention and wants him to go away. After that, the scent and sight of hawthorns in bloom has a disconcerting effect on him. Eventually, at the end of the book he meets the same girl, now a widow, with her daughter. He recalls the incident on the walk. She tells him that his interpretation of her gesture was completely wrong. It was meant to tell him that she wanted him. It was passionate. He had simply mistaken the passion. A new light breaks back onto the whole intervening story, re-evaluating the past and glamorizing with teasing significance the young daughter standing by, to whom the future belongs.

New Testament readers ought to take note of that story, or of the equivalents they are sure to have in their own experience. As they sift the gospel records for what is most historically true in them, they tend to work with a prejudice that the earliest is the best. Which is the earliest of the four gospels? What were the sources behind it? If only they could get through the text to the apostles who were there with Jesus, the objective truth of it all would be theirs. But they bang into a contradiction. Mark's is, by current consensus, the earliest of the gospels. yet in its pages Jesus' most intimate followers understand practically nothing of what Jesus says and does. The truth of it all is revealed only at the very end and to a character who has nothing to do with them: the centurion who, seeing Jesus die, says "Truly this was the Son of God" and so matches the title which Mark put as the first words of his book "The beginning of the gospel of Jesus Christ the Son of God" — a beginning which, as with Proust, we only get to at the end! To descend to a lower level, it is in any case a fact of experience, that eyewitnesses and early accounts have no privileged priority of truth. What they make available is open to other accountings. Our own childhood, the life and death of Jesus, the causes of the last war or the crusades — in principle, these can all be better understood now than they were at the time or at any intervening time; for example by advances in analytical techniques or the increase of information. They can also be understood worse: for example, by information being lost or the dominance of an inept ideology. And every understanding is revisable, even is bound to be revised, as part and parcel of our appropriating of anything that keeps on mattering to us.

The unconcluded and undecided story of the doctrine of the priesthood of women goes differently. There were no women priests in the New Testament churches. There were no men priests either. Priesthood, as far as they were concerned, was either a part of the officialdom of the Jerusalem temple which was lethally hostile to Jesus; or it was a heavenly state, belonging to the exalted Christ according to the epistle to the Hebrews or the saints in the heavenly Jerusalem according to the Revelation of John. The first Christians thought of it either too negatively or too positively to make it a part of their ordinary existence.

Christian priests came later. Before they existed, and in New Testament times, women were among the organizers of the household churches to which Paul wrote his letters. In the gospels women are among Jesus' followers, quite prominently in the gospels of Luke and John. Though they are not in "the twelve", they are chief witnesses of the crucial gospel events: Jesus' death and resurrection. In the current debate, supporters of the priesthood of women make full use of this, while their opponents try not to draw attention to the absence of priests from the first Christian churches. Neither of these moves is conclusive, but perhaps the supporters score a slight lead.

They soon lose it. Settling into Gentile culture, which was so creative for the doctrine of Christ as divine incarnation, was negative for the development of the role of women in the church. It was not so much the culture itself which held it back as the process of settling with its demand for strong structures of authority. There were, after all, women priests in Greek shrines and temples, such as there had never been in the Jewish temple – thus depriving women of the appeal to scriptural tradition which was so important in the formation of Christianity. It was as churches became more than private, domestic affairs and began to play an increasing part in the ordering of social life that they hardened into the patriarchal and male-dominated patterns of society at large. The priesthood and episcopate of men grew up with orthodoxy: a strong back to carry it, compared with the frail arrangements of Paul's little communities which were no longer suitable for a religion which was becoming a partner of secular authority.

But now, in our post-orthodox time, women priests are an option. How can we know whether to take it? The New Testament evidence is inconclusive. If Christianity had succeeded less, its women might have succeeded more, but "ifs" are not strong historical arguments. We need to think up some more productive questions. Religion being a practical concern, the questions need to be practical too. Would the priesthood of women be good for priesthood? Would it enhance the liveliness of the Christian tradition all together?

To answer the first of these two questions we need to pose the sort of questions which the selectors put to the current male candidates for priesthood (incidentally, not significantly different from the questions they put to female candidates for the diaconate). Are there women who have the deep and indispensable qualities required of priests, such as: sustained loyalty to historic tradition, the ability to think clearly and with practical imagination about the people and traditions they serve, piety, the love of God? We will only get answers by posing these questions to women ready to respond to them. But the overwhelming probability that there are such women, even the certainty of many people's experience that there are, make it reasonable and prudent to go ahead with the positive prospect that standards of practical priesthood would be enhanced by the substantial increase in the number of good people to choose from.

And would it be good for the Christian tradition at large and beyond the arrangement of its clergy? The previous example of the making of the doctrine of incarnation can aptly be brought in now. It showed how the Christian tradition benefited in both depth and clarity, in the development of its sense of identity, when it moved into territory which had previously been strange to it. A flock thrives on new pasture – so long as it is pasture and not woodland or desert. In the Old Testament there were neither women priests nor incarnation of God. But traditions, to live, must move on as well as remember. More than that, they must feed: not on any old thing, but on new things which they are ready for. Just as a twentieth-century western Christian may have been deeply influenced by the Sermon on the Mount, a few plays of Shakespeare and some basic ideas of modern science and psychology, so during its long history Christianity has absorbed Platonic, Aristotelian, idealist and existentialist philosophy, polyphonic and romantic music, hierarchical and egalitarian social patterns, even pagan shrines and religious festivals. It does not have a poor appetite or a weak digestive system. Its spectacular longevity can only be the result of its intuitive ability to feed well, to sense what is the next thing to digest and do so. If once Christianity developed strength by assimilating the male-led patterns of the society around it, it would follow that now that the public life around the church is no longer a male preserve and is none the worse for it, a positive response such as making women priests would be as proper and healthy as the previous one of making men priests. What is sauce for the goose may not always be sauce for the gander, but time can make it so. There could be a Christian time for women priests and it could be now. But for it to be Christian, it needs to latch on to something clear and strong in Christian tradition. In the nature of this case, it cannot be something fully realized or the argument would not be taking place at all. It must be a clear hint, a credible promise in the tradition which is waiting to be realized.

The energy of early Christianity was the liberating strength which it got from crossing conventional religious boundaries. It radiated from the central figure of the unofficial teacher who had died a slave's death and lived freely beyond it. It carried through Paul's refusal to notice any real difference between Jews and Gentiles. It stimulated his churches to innovative thoughts and behaviour which he himself had to rein in. And sooner rather than later, a good deal of reining in and steadying down was required. Thanks to Paul, the radical equality of Jews and Gentiles was achieved. Other equalities, also proclaimed by him, were not. Some of them were major, perhaps too big for the time being then. They included the abolition of the difference in status between slaves and free people, and of that between men and women. Before those could be achieved, Christianity had changed from being a dissident to being an established religion with a preference for stability. It took Christianity longer than it cares to remember to withdraw its collusion from slavery. It did not vanish from long-Christian Europe until the thirteenth century, and from its colonies only in the last century. The exclusion of women from priesthood and episcopate may still be in force, but with such a leisurely pace for the working out of the consequences of the gospel, long-standing does not mean permanence. And there were forces in early Christianity which were set to break it. Only now do we have the sort of society in which it looks odd *not* to respond positively to the twinkle in Paul's eye, the female presences at the cross and the grave where Christianity was born.

But should the church dance to the tunes which the secular band plays? The heroic moments of Christianity in this century have often been marked by firm refusals to do so, resisting totalitarian states of right and left and the slipshod negligences of less energetic regimes. Refusal and resistance, the ability to say "no", is as indispensable a part of growth as the ability to say "yes". Without both, we are not equipped to make choices. But ripeness is all, timing is integral. The figure of Dietrich Bonhoeffer is a paradigm of it. When a friend remonstrated with him for making the Nazi salute on some public occasion, he replied, unperturbed, that it was not the thing or the time on which to play one's last card and get arrested. There was work of resistance to do yet. Bonhoeffer had chosen to be a Christian after he had chosen to be a theologian: an order of options only possible in the post-orthodox world where Christianity can be understood and studied without any allegiance to it. After these two choices of an old fashioned profession and a venerable religion, he made his choice to grasp the modern world at its most acutely painful point by joining the resistance to Hitler. He was ready to play an active, even (revoking his previous pacifist convictions on the ground that history had overtaken them) violent part in it. Arrested and imprisoned after the failure of the July plot in 1944, he wrote a series of extraordinary letters to his friend Bethge. They are extraordinary because of his staunch refusal to freewheel with the impetus of his stand against the evil in the world. Rather than denounce it, or the people who had not been as brave as himself, he turned his critical energy on Christianity's tendency to home in on the world's evil and weakness. He took up the cudgels left by Nietzsche the atheist — as a committed believer. Christianity should endorse what is good and strong in the world. Piety should never drain or obliterate the enjoyment of life: cultural, sexual, political or intellectual. Rather it should be like a *cantus firmus* in a composition by Bach: the firm, leisurely-paced tune which upholds the brilliant melodies above it. He warned that if Christianity failed to make such positive responses, if it did not become strong in its power to serve and enable rather than depress, it would become the doomed enclave of a few survivors from the past with a taste for religion. Coming from the cell of a man imprisoned for his ability to resist and withstand secular evil, that has force.

Bonhoeffer's whole story is a contradiction of any notion that the Christian should either stand against the world or help it along as a consistent and invariable stance based on dogma. He and the world are both on the move, so choices and revisions are always demanded. Sometimes he affirms the way things are, sometimes he opposes it. As Nietzsche said, "A yes, a no, a straight line". Our choices are made on the move and we move by making choices. We do these two things together in a way ships' navigators do, by taking bearings ahead, behind and alongside. We examine how a yes or a no at this point would relate to the past course, how continuous or discontinuous with it it would be. This is affected by how we place ourselves right now vis-a-vis our future destination and the sidewinds of current pressure. To get there from here should we set a more, or less, curving course? Nor do we have an indefinite time for these calculations. The present moment is (changing the metaphor to auctions) going, going – gone. If we do not know how much we can afford or how much we want this lot, we cannot bid appropriately and will end up with things we did not want that much or without things which we wanted more than we realized.

All this, though we – as individuals and as churches – do it hundreds of times a day, is complicated. A lot of data is handled intuitively. But there is a simplicity to it if our intuition goes for one thing: quality. We can see it do that if we tell ourselves that we want to be able to say, in retrospect, that we did what was best (and no less) at the time. Every choice makes a change. Good choices make changes for the better and are practice for more such. But to be that they must aim at the good with such relaxed concentration that the good in us is activated by it: good looking and good thinking, clear affirmations and denials. In order to get some insight into that all-important process, the next chapter will look at painters at work.

4

Picture Making

Long before people got round to representing the world around them by writing, they did it with pictures. Anyone who has seen the cave paintings of Lascaux will have stood in front of masterpieces which reveal and challenge our prejudice that literacy and intellectual skill are coterminous. These paintings are the work of very clever people. We cannot recover the religion of the Lascaux painters, and so check the conviction of archeologists that they were religiously motivated. But to look at pictures as powerful as these – not just clever, but movingly alive – demands a response at the religious level, deeper than the top-of-the-head, snap reactions of assent or dissent which we can get away with in the face of verbal statements.

Between ourselves and reality we put systems of images. Perhaps we do it because real, raw life is not enough for us. Perhaps we do it because real, raw life is too much for us. Very likely we do it because it is both not enough and too much – and so make representations of it on which we can reflect and let our unsatisfied and over-filled minds play at leisure. Anyhow, we do it. Between ourselves and noise we put music. Between ourselves and the mobile clutter of things we put pictures. We are like Tennyson's Lady of Shalott, who wove away at her loom and saw the world refracted by a mirror. Like her, should we look directly at the world and see an actual Sir Lancelot approaching over the fields, catastrophe occurs. The mirror shatters and the weaving unravels. Then we are lost: for good or ill, for the time being or forever.

For fear of this sort of thing happening, most of us, most of the time, live carefully to Shalott rules. We get religion to help us do so. We subordinate everything to the picture of the world which we have hung up over the mental hearth, or which we are busy weaving. We see only, as St Paul said, reflections in a mirror or "through a glass darkly". Going down a street, we do not see the street. We obliterate it by the labels we have stuck on, and check cursorily as we go: "the chemist's, manhole, Jack's house". Rich complexities of light and shade, weird juxtapositions of shapes, majestic spaces – these are all screened out. So we make sense of sorts, and take the person who stops and stares for some kind of eccentric idler.

And then comes the painter. He or she is in the same game: or worse, considering how a painter is moulded by an art-school training, pressed upon by dealers who know what the rest of us will buy because it will confirm our prejudices. So the painter makes no difference, but just adds another image to the infinite lumber room of images. Such painters make no difference precisely because they alter the world to suit their strong internal images. Which is what we all do anyhow.

But it could always be different. Every blank canvas or piece of paper taken up, raises the wonderful possibility that some reality, some life-direct, might get onto it. Then, though mirror shatters and work-to-date unravels, familiar techniques get kicked into new vivacity and truth. It is this possibility, which has been realized in masterpieces, which we are looking out for. It happens in a moment of transition which is also a moment of transubstantiation near to the heart of the Christian eucharist. Something happens at the tip of a brush which makes person or tree into paint, paint into person or tree. Thinking has gone out to the edge of flesh. It has made a bit of reality available and assimilable to other, ordinarily mirror-dominated, people. They are surprised and delighted by it. Because there is real presence there is also communion. That is why it is like the ritual moment when Christ becomes bread and wine, bread and wine become Christ. It is the exchange that has made Life (the capital L meaning that life has been enlarged in two senses: set free and increased) available to people who are only "living and partly living". So the contemplation of great pictures gives us a grateful sense of being well fed. We want to say some sort of grace.

It is worth looking a little harder at how this possibility comes about.

The painter turns from his usual mirror to look at the world. This is a difficult and dangerous switch, like the transitions from singleness to marriage or from marriage to parenthood which most of us make — with proper trepidation. As we are supported at these moments by religious tradition, so the painter is comforted by pictorial tradition. This means that the way to the magic moment is not at all magical. It is the long, traditional routine of learning a craft, so thoroughly that in the end it has entered one's body. It comes down from the forebears and contemporaries who have similarly dared and got to this crucial point. But those who get there are on their own. "This is my body" — a terribly solitary point. Firmly and gently, the tradition pushes you out to the front where you are alone, face to face with the unassimilated, unknown and unmapped. You feel, perhaps, like a lion-tamer, or the victim of the legendary Turkish torture who is locked into a cell with a homicidal maniac who will kill him if he once takes his eye off him. Negligence or panic will be instantly punished by a bad mark, right there on the canvas or paper. The vain wish to paint a good picture will be punished by a bad one. Time ticks by, and the painter works with time, sensing when to act and when to wait. His eye and his hand go together, always up to two things.

The first is sharp. Gimlet eye and pointed tool probe and analyse. The painter is a critic, dividing unities, dismembering structures. According to the epistle to the Hebrews the creative word of God is like that, a sword dividing joints and marrow.

The second is soft. Bedroom eye and flexing tool caress and fondle. The painter is an admiring lover who does not want to break or change things but to accept and leave everything exactly as it is. According to the gospel of Luke, Mary's quiet listening to Jesus, while her sister Martha was busy chopping and cleaning in the kitchen, was that "good part which shall not be taken away".

The combination of the passive with the active means that the whole of the painter's mind and body is engaged in his work. The concentration which demands everything makes the painter fully himself in the very business of forgetting himself to attend to his subject. A gospel promise is honoured: he who loses his life finds it, and more. He who gets lost out of the world of known images achieves a new, true image. In New Testament language, he has changed from a slave to a son, a fellow worker with the Creator who knows what the Creator is doing by participation in the work. Passivity and activity, combined in self-forgetfulness for the sake of the glory set before him, has made the painter more than a slavish imitator of nature. Vincent Van Gogh testified to this in a letter to his brother.

A man's head or a woman's head, well observed and at leisure, is divinely beautiful, isn't it? Well, one *loses* that *general harmony* by painfully exact imitation; one *keeps* it by recreating in a parallel colour-scale which may not be exactly, or even far from exactly, like the model.

There is help there for those who are puzzled by green heads in modern painting, or by bread body in traditional ritual. The painter can make marks which are not exact imitations but something more alive – free parallels, real *re*-presentations. For they have a real presence in them. This is because he has let his body – mind, heart, eye and hand obviously, but he feels it in his toes and up his spinal column too – be the passage through which alien particularities are reborn into wide meanings. Entering a room in a gallery we can say immediately "Cezanne!" as truly as if we had bumped into the old man himself. For we have. He is more recognizably present in his work than in his person, which we might mistake for one of his similarly-bearded contemporaries such as Freud. But this moment of instant recognition is only possible because Cezanne was not busy being Cezanne. He was inviting apples, bottles and table-cloth into the recognizability of real presence by the sharpness and softness of his gaze and the total dedication to *them* of his body. We can say "Cezanne!" so confidently because he, under his breath said "apple". In each case the tone was of greeting, of annunciation.

Christ, old doctrine says, is really present in the sacrament which holds, in bread and wine, what his body suffered and achieved: the life and death he had to greet, what he had passively let happen and what he had actively made happen. Here too, particularities grasped and affirmed have their dreadful rawness changed into useful and manageable significance, their solitariness changed into the company of a *sacrum convivium*. Death was taken on: the terrible reality which daunts us all, most alien yet natural moment of deconstruction. And the taking on of it meant life for other bodies. Van Gogh wrote of Christ, whom he had served first as a preacher, and then more as a painter:

> He lived serenely, as a greater artist than other artists, despising marble and clay as well as colour, working in living flesh.

If that puts Christ above the artists, at the same time it puts him with all human beings, including artists, who try to make something meaningful out of their lives and have only their bodies to do it with. It connects the business of art with the business of moral living.

It is a connection which is not always made and is often denied. Artists, like their admirers, are as glad as the rest of us for leave to forget the demands of being good. Perhaps the creative goodness of their work allows them to waste their personal lives and spoil the lives of the people around them. Yeats thought that they were faced with a straight choice between perfection of the life or of the work. Christians have to question that sort of division in the name of human wholeness. When they go to church they take part in ceremonies with a strong and indispensable input of art: music, formal movement, costumes, colour and architecture. But while they attend positively to all this, they also attend to a continual moral insistence which is at work all the time, getting them to learn by their rituals how to repent, forgive and be good – to one another and to the others who are not there. They are held and trained in a unity of the artistic and the moral which bind together in the presence of Christ. They respond to it by believing that goodness is indivisible.

This does not give them any excuse for setting themselves apart from artists by means of a hard-faced and judgemental pharisaism, usually masking indolent philistinism. "Judge not, and ye shall not be judged." Artists put themselves at risk whenever they are really creative, because it requires them to cross the boundaries of hitherto ordered experience and get to terms with the wilderness. This happens to all of us in our critical times of transitional change. Then we want wise support, not condemnation; sympathy, not indifference. We can only say that artists come under the same moral rules as the rest of us if we realize that we are in the same moral dangers as they, that each needs the other's help in the business of understanding our common human life.

It is help which has to be given and taken on the move: a goodness which grows, adapts and is fertile.

This need of help given and taken on the move puts into question the static picture of goodness as a sort of cake — that favourite accounting metaphor in a time when accountants rule: what I have, you cannot have; what is used for this (art) cannot be used for that (morals). This is not a satisfactory metaphor, even on its own financial terms. Money which is imaginatively looked after, firmly and adaptably managed, becomes fertile, breeding more money and confounding simplistic cake-slicers. A business with any human imagination soon realizes that misery at home undermines efficiency at work, that good work conditions do wonders for domestic life. Things move, bleed into one another, transform themselves by exchange, and set off new ventures.

Christianity is impeded by obstinately static pictures of the Christian paradigm of help, the presence of Christ. One such is to think of it as a nut. Crack the shell and discard it, then inside is the pure kernel which is Christ. This image has guided a lot of study of the gospels. Critics have spotted what the early Church contributed to them by noticing traces of its problems and solutions. They mark the traces of each evangelist, his favourite words, phrases and topics. Get rid of this extraneous stuff, they have supposed, and the authentic words of Christ will emerge in pristine purity. It has not worked, because the guiding metaphor was inadequate. It failed to take in the fertility of what Christ did and said, immediately and irrevocably germinating in lives not his. A better metaphor was right there in the texts they were studying, handed to them on the sacred plate. In the thirteenth chapters of both Matthew and Luke is a little parable.

> The kingdom of heaven is like unto leaven (yeast) which a woman took, and hid in three measures of meal, till it was all leavened.

Christ is everywhere in the gospel bread, but nowhere isolable or extractable from the meal of early Christian life. This is an energetic metaphor. Goodness, and the help which it gives, live by being consumed, digested and changed into other shapes. The more active it is, the more hidden and blended it is. It thrives on participation and exchange.

The Bible teems with such metaphors of the divine presence which is the world's best help. It has folk tales of inexhaustible meal-tubs and oil-jars, of a few loaves and fishes which, broken by the right hands, became banquets for thousands in the wilderness. Chief of them all is Moses' burning bush, God present in something consumed by fire yet not destroyed. These are appropriately creative pictures of creativity itself. St Paul described that creativity in more personal terms when he wrote of himself and his colleagues as "afflicted in every way, but not crushed; perplexed but not driven to despair; persecuted but not forsaken; struck down, but not destroyed; always carrying in the body the death of Jesus, so that the life of Jesus may also be manifested in our bodies" (2 Corinthians 4:8-10 RSV). By being in the crucible of transformation, his body became a picture, a manifestation of divine power for other people. He was like Shadrach, Meshach and Abednego in the Book of Daniel. In the fire they sang the praises of creation: of air, water, birds, beasts, plants and people, and even fire itself. There was a fourth with them, the story goes, who was "like the Son of the Gods" – a figure of divine help. Were they aware of him? It does not say. Perhaps not. Van Gogh in his fiery torment as man and painter was not. But he was aware of the world's terrible beauty and of his own creativity.

> I can very well do without God but I cannot, ill as I am, do without something which is greater than I, which is my life – the power to create.

His distinction between "God" and the creativity "which is greater than I" collapses under the truth of what the biblical images tell of divine presence in the world. It is not needed if God is present as a creative genetic code in the world, absent as one quite apart from it. The second concept may be true. We will look into its truth in the next chapter. But the first is our business, or rather, that ground of our business which we are not conscious of as we throw ourselves into our work. The Christian doctrine of divine Trinity sees divine life as a continual self-transforming change which gathers all life into itself and radiates it out as grace and healing. The sacrament of the eucharist puts it to us as bread to be shared. It is an image of the divine art which is our life. And we learn it.

5

Acknowledging Darkness

In Van Gogh's last pictures café interiors glare with hellish light, cypress trees burn like flames, and over the harvest fields black crows flap and inky cloud lowers. Our central theme of consumption is terrible as well as happy. The faith that goodness is indivisible always operates under the threat of break-up and within the ordeal of history and of evil.

In historical existence everything is subject to change and decay. "The grass withereth, the flower fadeth." Good people die, the people on whom we have depended for our moral nourishment. Often we have killed them. And even good ideas, although they last longer than their thinkers, can fall apart under the pressure of temporal circumstances. Great artists become such by accepting this as implicit to everything they do. They cannot rest on their laurels. To have just done something well puts them in danger, and they sense it. For they cannot stop there. Time goes on. The next work beckons. Will they be up to it? Their proper trepidation is itself a temptation to fall back on old techniques and ideas which have worked well before. Succumbed to, it will result in second-rate work, deprived of the alert attention, the creative trepidation, which made good work before. Every new work is a new beginning, putting the maker in jeopardy all over again, a post-ponement of failure. It is the same in moral and religious life. To have been a good wife, husband, child, workmate, or employer so far is to land oneself in the same testing predicament. The next encounter with husband, wife, parent or whoever, will require yet again the open alertness of starting afresh. To inherit a great religious tradition like Christianity will require the open alertness of discovering it afresh, not the stylized repetition of an old manner deprived of the attentive spirit which once made it good. And whatever the context, this time we might be facing something less tractable and digestible than before. It could be the end of the line.

A realistic sense of the strength of evil awakens terror at every new beginning. Not only does time wither the rose. That is not so much evil as sad. Evil means something worse.

> O rose, thou art sick:
> The invisible worm
> That flies in the night,
> In the howling storm,
> Has found out thy bed
> Of crimson joy;
> And his dark secret love
> Does thy life destroy.

WILLIAM BLAKE: Songs of Experience XIII

Human beings are not just the victims of the destructions brought about by external fortune. They also destroy out of the forces within themselves which spring from a deep and secret hatred of life, a dark love.

Sooner or later we have to face this, a trial which we may not survive – in our nuclear and nature-wasting time, all too literally. It is the destiny of goodness to face it. Such is the basic and shaping conviction of the gospel of Mark.

That story begins with a powerful injection of good energy, worked out in healings and lives restored. But this passes inevitably, and sooner than careless readers may notice, into the phase where the story is dragged forward by the bleak certainty of disaster. Jesus announces, more than once, that he will be betrayed, rejected and killed. His followers, naturally not wanting to hear this, therefore cannot understand it. But for him it is a necessity, a destiny written into his story as its God-given genetic code. And he goes to it open-eyed. It began far back. "Judas Iscariot, which also betrayed him" was one of the twelve he chose to share his work at its outset (Mark 3:13). When, eventually, Judas goes about his business of betrayal, the menacing note of necessity is repeated, confirmed by sacred scripture. Jesus says at the last supper:

> The Son of Man goes as it is written of him, but woe to that man by whom the Son of Man is betrayed! It would have been better for that man if he had not been born. (Mark 14:21)

There speaks the tragic conviction. The doom of Jesus is not solitary but is set off by, and sets off, the doom of another man. This had to happen. Yet Judas is culpable. An aboriginal flaw, long latent and running way back beyond Judas' childhood, now fractures as pressure is brought to bear. Yet he is responsible. The paradox of fate and responsibility is real. We recognize it as part of our lives whenever we are faced by the moral ambiguity which fuels our living: for example when a successful vicar or social-worker recognizes that his work has not only been done at the expense of his own family, but even energized by a secret recoil from family intimacy. It sent him out to deal with people who gave him more status and control. Behind the love was a hidden indifference, even hatred. This is tragic. To recognize it is hard, though doing so is an inescapable stage in the process of healing. Shakespeare's Prospero can only return to civil society as a healed healer when he has accepted his monster-helper Caliban with "this thing of darkness I acknowledge mine". Before the Freudian analyst is allowed to catalogue the murderous and incestuous contents of the cellars of other personalities, he must have itemized his own. Tragedy, recognized, makes us wise. With what sort of wisdom?

In ancient Greece, where it was born, tragedy had a civic setting. It was part of political and religious life. It was a good work, a public benefaction expected of rich men, to sponsor performances of the great tragedians Aeschylus, Euripides and Sophocles. Needless to say, our bouncily money-oriented politicians today minimize (they do not quite disown) that sort of responsibility. The terrible stories of the Greek theatre were enacted as an integral part, as integral as roads or defence, of how people live together and of how divinity and humanity interrelate. They were representations of the social and religious reality which their participants, players and patrons, all inhabited. Taking part in them, whether as sponsor, performer or audience, was an assertion, by being there all day, that the recognition of tragedy is necessary for strong community binding. That was its wisdom. And Mark, the Christian evangelist, shared it. His narrative, with all its dark secrets, fractures and assault on complacency, was a book for a community. It was to be read aloud, performed, at its gatherings. There the last supper, Judas included, was re-enacted to reinforce participation in the dark mystery.

Why, though, do we feel better for taking part in things

like this? It is easy and proper enough to enjoy art which represents what is happy in life. Is it perverse, even ghoulish or pretentious, to enjoy art which represents what is appalling? Our experience is that we come away from *King Lear* or *King Oedipus* with a sense that the shock we have fielded has done us good, pleased by the truth of the representation. We understand better how things are with us, and converse animatedly. It has got us together with a strength shared by happier occasions only when they are as searching and untoward. We are more sober and responsible. We have allowed ourselves to "feel what wretches feel". We have become wiser in the ground of our whole seeing of the world, and so in a quite practical way. Tragic wisdom, which begins with art's appeal to feelings, is practical and moral in the end.

To those who have faced tragedy, forgiveness is more possible. They have shared a glimpse of the misfortune and the evil which we have in common. They have seen Dostoyevsky's truth that "we are all responsible for everything and for everyone." Condemnation is much more suspect now, because they have assented to its truth. This, after all, is where we begin if we can take it. Tragic performances give us practice and a dry run. The ordinary world with its pride and pomps, with that optimism which cruelly blames others for anything which upsets it, does little or nothing to help us take it. But tragedy has recognized and unmasked that too. Tragedy, like religion and because it is religious, has done something to steady us and get us to take it all. Its deepest religious wisdom is to tell us that our continual attempts to dissociate ourselves from what is bad and awful only fasten us into its coils more thoroughly, like frantic birds trying to escape from a net. The very fact that tragedies and gospels are representations, aside from actuality, give us the relaxed detachment and secluded space (the theatre, the church) which recognition needs. The recognition itself can enable us, like Prospero, to be released and to release others. Jesus' close but detached (because free) association with publicans and sinners, the outcast little tragedies of society, was an integral part of his healing way.

This is a dangerous idea which walks along a knife edge. Everything depends on the attitude or spirit of the walker – as ever. To espouse the tragic idea as something which will work like magic and bring us fame, brings an immediate fall into the sentimentality or the cruelty which are always at the elbow of those who deal with tragedy. It is looking, with steady concentration, at the focus of affliction, which keeps us upright.

There is a remarkable story about such looking in the book of Numbers (chapter 21). In the course of the forty-year ordeal of wandering in the wilderness which brought the Israelites to the Promised Land, they were attacked by deadly snakes. As a medicine, God told Moses to make a snake in bronze and put it up on a pole in the middle of the camp. "If a serpent bit any man, he would look at the bronze serpent and live" (21.9). It is a precise image of the homeopathic therapy which comes from facing an image of the source of suffering. And it uses a representation, as distinct from the real thing which was going on among them, to do it. When Perseus killed the monster Gorgon he was guided by its image on the polished inside face of his shield, because its direct gaze would have (literally) petrified him. The mirror-shield of art is here not an evasion but necessary protection for those getting at the real, and dreadful, thing. Mathis Grünewald did the same for the plague hospital at Isenheim when he painted his horrifying crucifixion as a representation of mortal affliction for the dying to look at and be helped. John, the Christian evangelist, had made the connection which Grünewald explored. He joined Moses' bronze serpent to Jesus' crucifixion. "As Moses lifted up the serpent in the wilderness, so must the Son of Man be lifted up, that whosoever believes in him may have eternal life" (John 3.14). The acknowledgement of affliction, of the negative against life which is death, became positive by being given sacred value. And this value could only be given by means of representation. The thing itself, the plague which ravaged the people of Israel or of Isenheim, was only negative. The representation of it was a countervailing positive act with positive effect.

Grünewald's painting was made to stand over the altar where priests represented the death of Christ which made the outcast worshippers into a holy communion. Christ was among the sick again, as the "thing of darkness" (not forgetting Judas, the betrayer recalled at every eucharist) was acknowledged. People who confessed their belonging in the society of darkness and fatality were able to find their place in the society of light and life. On the other side of Grünewald's crucifixion was his resurrection, Christ restored and escaping the heavy stone of his tomb.

Tragedy and eucharist are representations which enforce on us our participation in death. And our culpability too. They bring us into an association which is the opposite of the optimistic demand that society should be cleansed of its negative elements — the sinners or the moribund — in order to be flourishing and worth belonging to. That is dissociation which, ironically but inevitably, effects no cure but only compounds affliction. Everybody feels its pull. We would like to get back to the Garden of Eden — without its snake. Utopias and cocksure religious sects beckon. Believing ourselves to be innocent but misunderstood, we idly and cruelly imagine that if a few negative people could be got out of the way — left-wing elements, bourgeois reactionaries, Jews or theological Judases who betray the gospel — we would soon be walking back to the paradise garden. The results of acting on that dream are familiar to our century and marked at Auschwitz and Katin, by Senator McCarthy and by Pol Pot. The eucharist is crucially important because it speaks of better things. Beginning with tragic reality rather than flattering dream, it fosters communion rather than crusade.

When returns to Eden are proposed, it is worth remembering Edwin Muir. He was, according to his *Autobiography*, born into the paradise of an Orkney farm where man and nature were at one. Poverty forced him and his family out of it. After a period of admiring Nietzsche's philosophy of the ruthless pursuit of health, he espoused Christianity. It reconciled his experience of paradise, certainly not innocence restored, but the responsible compassion required and given in his marriage. He celebrated it in poetry.

> Time takes the foliage and the fruit
> And burns the archetypal leaf
> To shapes of terror or of grief
> Scattered along the winter way.
> But famished field and blackened tree
> Bear flowers in Eden never known.
> Blossoms of grief and charity
> Bloom in these darkened fields alone.
> What had Eden ever to say
> Of hope and faith and pity and love

Until was buried all its day
And memory found its treasure trove?
Strange blessings never in Paradise
Fall from these beclouded skies.

EDWIN MUIR: "One Foot in Eden"

First he sees tragedy as the effect of time and guilt. But its winter has flowers: grief naturally, but also, supernaturally, charity. Eden had to go and be buried with its innocence. It did not need the adult love, faith and hope which are needed now. Only when it became a memory rather than actuality did these "strange blessings" flourish on its grave. Blessing after disaster and acknowledging disaster, is kinder and wiser than innocence. It is the only way we can be together now, and the only realistic hope.

Hope, faith and love: Muir got these virtues from the famous thirteenth chapter of 1 Corinthians. So his source was the extraordinary outburst of religious creativity which was early Christianity. We have already seen something of it in its bright aspects. What we have seen in this chapter suggests that this was a vitality born out of disaster and the acknowledgement of darkness. If faith, hope and love are fully themselves and not weak excuses for other things, they are the virtues of exiles from Eden who know they cannot get back there.

In New Testament times, as now, people became Christians by being baptized. But then it was a grimmer rite, its formality framing an adult, tragic apprehension rather than infant joy. "Know ye not", asked Paul, "that as many of us as were baptized into Jesus Christ were baptized into his death?" He knew what he was talking about. His own life was, as he felt it, a carrying about in his body of Jesus' dying (2 Corinthians 4:10). It was the secret of his courage and charity, the source of his ability to make communities in his world. The tragic assent was primary. Without it there could be nothing, and religious eloquence or shrewdness were no substitutes.

> And I, brethren, when I came to you, came not with excellency of speech or of wisdom, declaring unto you the testimony of God. For I determined not to know anything among you save Jesus Christ, and him crucified. (1 Corinthians 2:2)

Christ's crucifixion was for Paul the sum of all tragedy. It was the loss of all that had been painfully achieved in religion, in the moment when the fracture which ran through the human world, beginning with Adam, broke the Son of God. This was *the* transition in which Christ's crossing over from the territory of his native innocence enabled the guilty to cross over into the good land (2 Corinthians 5:21) — but only, and strictly, if they experienced in their own bodies the death of Christ by way of its representation in the baptismal rite of passage. And Paul spoke of that representation in strong language of participation; dying with Christ and being buried with him.

And then resurrection. But when, exactly? Not yet. For Paul resurrection was eschatological, something reserved for the end of the world. Paul thought that end was close. The resurrection was no further ahead of him than the death was behind him. Neither being remote, he lived in the field of force between the two. The dying of baptism went on, the revival at the end was so close that he could "walk in newness of life" (Romans 6:4) already — its vital light was on the path. We do not usually feel time with such compactness. It takes a tragic play or a church ritual to do

71

it for us. Then, in an hour or two, we can be taken through the full pattern which originally took far longer. Human origins and ends are pressed on us more closely. It is meant to change our lives, to work out in moral adjustments inspired by it — which also take far longer. With Paul, the death and life which were compressed into baptism, had to be worked out in long-winded and painstaking detail. But all the detail could be put under two headings. The first was the making way for others which is defined by death. The second was the freedom from religious and secular norms which was to be defined by resurrection. Such a life of liberated responsibility, of giving way and going ahead, was a continual transition. He was utterly obliged to Christ and his neighbours and utterly free. That was what the tragedy of the cross had done for him.

6

Personal, Apersonal and Communion

But now you will ask me "How am I to think of God himself, and what is he?" and I cannot answer you except to say "I do not know!" For with this question you have brought me into the same darkness, the same cloud of unknowing, where I want you to be! For though we through the grace of God can know fully all about other matters, and think about them — yes, even the very works of God himself — yet of God himself can no man think. Therefore I will leave on one side everything I can think, and choose for my love that thing which I cannot think! Why? Because he may well be loved, but not thought. By love he can be caught and held, but by thinking never.

The Cloud of Unknowing

Knowledge of God is not something which floats about, free of time and easily available on not-very-serious demand. It happens at the moments in time which are characterized by something of the transitional ordeal. Tragedy was not just there at the beginning of Christianity. It is an indication of the seriousness demanded of any attempt to do theology that tragedy is with it all the time, accompanying it wherever it goes. If theological textbooks have concealed that under a certain glibness or joviality, the biographies of believers make it very clear. They knew

73

about God when they lost a lot and found a lot, when obligation and freedom became real and actual for them. They lived in transition. And whatever they did or said was, they knew, failure as much as achievement, matter for penitence as much as praise. It was never quite adequate and always liable to fatal misuse as it fell into the hands of wicked, or just lazy, men — or people as fallible as themselves. We will find an insoluble tragic element however we try to talk about God. Sooner or later anything we say will come apart, and failure to acknowledge that will result in cruel or decadent theology.

To take up the task: how can we think of God? Anything worthwhile, anything worthy of the subject, will not come about just in the top of the head and be an adroit manoeuvring of airy notions. It will involve our whole selves. Not least, it will involve our imaginations and our behaviour, to which images are more fundamental than notions. So we will be dealing in the images, or symbols, which persuade us at depth and to which notions are critical commentary. Our imagining and behaving selves are not static. So thinking about God in which we are thoroughly engaged will be a series of timed movements, a choreography or log of navigation, rather than a single or stable utterance. It will be more like a rite than a monument. The thinking will be a matter of watching our step — three steps, in fact, which will go something like this.

First, we will begin with imagining God as person. Finding a flaw in this, we will at least want to counteract it. Secondly, we will treat the counteractions as worthwhile resources in their own right — not just as protests against something else — and entertain the opposite idea of God as impersonal. We will find that this, too, has lethal tendencies. So thirdly, having recognized the dangers in

both of these and retreated just in time, we will settle for
something which looked less settled than either of them
but is really our home ground: the mediation of divinity
by the Christ present in holy communion which includes
the acknowledgement of tragedy.

We make gods in our own image. Apparently this is the
best we can do, but people have been uneasy with it since
the Old Testament prophets at least. Other people's
religions have been the usual training ground of critical
theology. There, feelings of unease with religion can be
turned into tools of polemical criticism for use on other
people's gods. They are idols, artefacts, mere representations without lives of their own. "Look, this is how they
make them!"

> The smith with the tongs both worketh in the coals,
> and fashioneth it with hammers, and worketh it with the
> strength of his arms ... He maketh a god, even his
> graven image: he falleth down unto it and worshippeth
> it. (Isaiah 44: 10-18)

More drastic and generous religious thinkers have grasped
the nettle of realizing that what is sauce for the heathen
goose is also sauce for the orthodox gander. They have
turned their awareness of the anthropomorphic element in
theology onto their own theological thinking, putting it
through the critical ordeal previously reserved for others.
Ezekiel did this in the great and complex image of God
which occupies the first chapters of his book. He presented
a human image which he continually burned and twisted
with qualifications: realism put in question by surrealism.
The God he saw was "a likeness as it were of human form".
But this quasi-human being was made of "as it were

gleaming bronze", and yet was "like the appearance of fire". Contradictions are set against one another. God is something like a person. But God is unlike human persons because made of much more durable stuff: bronze. But no, he is made of more transient and evanescent stuff than we: fire.

Ezekiel's wariness with anthropomorphism is common coin in the modern study of religion. Thanks to much practice in sizing up various religions by seeing what they do for their societies, we can soon see what a strongly personal image of God usually does for people. It makes order. If God is personal, then he must be like the most important kind of person known, a king. Think of him so, and you bring needed order into that wild and woolly anarchy which makes religion so creative but so socially dangerous. Question that thought, as the early Christians did when they told of Jesus as king when he became the lowest sort of person, the dying outcast of the crucifixion, and you question that order and become no dependable friend of Caesar.

We have come to notice this nowadays because the present is a time when personal images of God are having a thin time anyway. Their whole context has shrunk and been destabilized. There have been deep and pervasive changes in the picture of the world which once formed the theatre of operations of the old personal god. Room for his grand interventions has shrunk as more and more of it has been taken over by human technology for human purposes. His native marshes have been made into market gardens, his forests felled to make pastures for domestic animals and paper for book production. These are, themselves, questionable activities which need criticism. But they raise daunting questions too. How do gods who have lost so much territory survive? If there were no Churches or Christians, would the Christian God still be there? These are not merely saucy questions. People who have been brave enough to face their own mortality, their own tragedy, have also been able to face this fear. For as long as people have sensed the divine they have also dreaded the passing away of their gods.

There is logic in the fear. If gods are persons like us, then they must have biographies like ours. The best known one is the story of the Norse god Wotan, as told by Wagner in *The Ring*. It is tragic. Wotan was strongly personal, ruling the world by covenants engraved on his all-powerful spear. But these covenants tangled into his marital life with Fricka, and so into his own inner life of thought and feeling. It was precisely his caring rule over the human world, the quality of his monarchy, which entangled him in its evil. Such implication is the very stuff of tragedy, here taken into the destiny of personal divinity.

This is a powerful warning, giving urgency and energy to the efforts of Christian theologians to counteract the personal image of deity and stabilize it by drastic checks on the fatal tendency of thorough-going images of God as person to come to grief.

We can see these correctives at work if we recall traditional Christian paintings of God in heaven. He sits on his throne, the eternal and ageless one in the image of a man in vigorous but calm late middle-age. Around him are other persons, also paradoxically represented. They are engaged in rapturous musical praise. Music is the most time-dependent of the arts (no time, no music), yet the one most capable of taking us out of time. It serves praise because praise is an ecstatic state in which we go out of ourselves and our own time and knowledge, to be lost in the joy of acknowledging an other, the Other. Yet these heavenly people, while carried away, stand in perfect and stable order. If we can imagine such a thing, happy abandonment is their steady state. Ritual is as near to it as we can get. One thing, at any rate, is clear. Like Ezekiel, the painters of these pictures took care to provide impersonal correctives to their personal images. They were aware, and want to tease us into seeing, that this is another world than our usual world of persons. They face us with persons who are apersonal because selfless. They simultaneously represent and question the personal in the divine realm.

There is moral, as well as aesthetic, point to their resistance against headlong commitment to personality in the divine. At the human end, destructive forces are at work in the making of personal gods. Isaiah noticed them in his idol-maker, breaking up perfectly good natural materials to make a supernatural nonentity which was a waste of people's time and best feelings. Feuerbach and his more famous disciple Karl Marx noticed these destructive forces in more recent representers of God. The first move of these image-makers was to throw out or project themselves, making a God in their own likeness, slightly improved. Then, having forgotten or hidden this imaginative effort, they worshipped its congenial, but alienated, product. Their fault was the fatal split in the world which their theological imagination had made. It began with a split in themselves, by which their best gifts and hopes were disowned and put on to "God". Then it carried into splits in social life, estranging them from their neighbours – who cryingly needed the love and goodness which they had directed elsewhere. Neighbours got treated as ways and means, not ends. Something bad had happened to love when anyone, even oneself, was treated like that. The Christian who believes that God is love is well aware that something had gone wrong. As neighbours to other faiths, or to deviants within their own faith, Christians were at their unloving worst when they were strongest in their belief in a strongly personal God.

They are not so bad now, and not so strong in this sort of theology. But they see the tragedy of their own past played out again before them in the tragedy of the contemporary fundamentalist revivals. How has faith in a merciful and compassionate God become associated with terror and torture as means of justice? The pure otherness of God has become contaminated with all-too-human notions of will. There has been an overloading of personality and personal will on to divinity which has left human persons as casualties and made God disreputable.

If personal divinity has these tendencies, even in such great traditions as Christianity and Islam, we ought to value the remedies against them highly enough to make them the starting point for new beginnings. We should give a hearing to the most radical ideas of how different God is from people like us.

Religion speaks of another, a quite other, reality. If it does not, it disappears into the secular — as the over-personal theologies so dreadfully do. There is a bold assertion of the difference between God and us in the first of the Church of England's *Thirty-nine Articles of Religion*. It says that God is without a body, parts or passions. God does not have what constitutes our own personalities. God is other. Mystics, in Islam and Christianity, have taken this more seriously and positively than ecclesiastical theologians have done, so providing hopeful alternatives to their efforts.

They do not have such big holdings or duties in the public ordering of religion. Situated at its edge in their cells and hermitages, they take a way of inner purification, along which the critique of personal images of God, even their loss, has been the way to union with God. Their deconstruction of theology's personal symbolism has not been disengaged or easy, but accompanied all the way by their deconstruction of self towards resolution in a deep and dazzling darkness: a place beyond the world and its diseases. The rest of us protect ourselves by raging against that night. They are its friends and call it good. Only if we are so badly hurt as to be sick and tired of the world do we feel inclined to follow them. Then we,

> ... long for scenes which man has never trod,
>   A place where women never smiled or wept;
> There to abide with my creator, God.
>   And sleep as I in childhood sweetly slept.

JOHN CLARE: "I am"

With similar revulsion, Wagner turned from contemplating Wotan's self-defeat to the other world beyond personality and its death. In Act III of *Tristan and Isolde* the hero, wounded by his amorous entanglement in the ordinary world, wakes from the long coma induced by his wound. His squire congratulates him on being at home in his own castle again. But Tristan does not feel at home there, or anywhere in the world. In his unconsciousness he has been elsewhere. He cannot describe it. He saw no land, no people. Yet it was where he had always been, where he had always been going. He called it, lamely, the great realm of cosmic night. It was the world inside out. God? Atheism? Or the ultimate truth of God beyond the personal?

Whatever it was, we may well feel as disconcerted by the way this is going as we were by the way personal theology went. Is this good for us either? Here is the other world which religion must affirm. But it is, of its nature, not cashable in our world of urgent duties to neighbours and families. It bankrupts it. Along this trail our innermost longing for life is transformed into an inner desire for death and beyond. So Wagner himself described the drama of *Tristan*. It is sufficient reason for steering clear of it. This sort of thing threatens to infect healthy earthly life with germs from outer space which baffle our immune systems. It will not do for the living. Because we are personal and our lives are unconcluded, we cannot rest in the ultimate and impersonal. We should face it. There is a road which ends there. Don't all roads end there? But then we should go about the penultimate affairs which are the business of penultimate people like us. From the graveside or the crematorium we go back to tea and sympathy, ordinary society or ordinary solitude.

Two disappointments. But we have not been wasting time, going up cul-de-sacs at the end of which were frights from which we had to retreat, none the wiser. We are wiser, because we have faced, not just frights, but tragic truths. The first was the inevitability of historical process and the accompanying implication in the world's guilt which works on persons and on personal theology. The second was the otherness, beyond personality, of God. We have seen how things go. We have acknowledged human and divine darkness.

The value of this in religious terms is the fundamental and traditional religious value of facing death. For Paul, it was indispensable. It matters crucially. Death is the mediator between worlds. It is the place where we hand over to one another our material and spiritual goods. It is the mark of transitoriness which we cannot rub out, which fixes our betwixt-and-betweenness. Death's inescapable paradox is that it is so very much us, written into our leases of life, and yet something very much other which we survive by postponing.

In Christian thinking, death has the crucial value of the dying with Christ which happens in the midst of our unconcluded biographies, making them Christian and better. The paradox of dying so as to live is solved by symbols like Moses' brazen serpent or the actions of the priest at the altar. A representation of death, something which is not exactly death itself but which by standing for it brings some of its effect home to our imaginations before we die, is the only way we can assimilate this truth without it finishing us off. Passed through the lens of representation, the power of death which would otherwise be totally annihilating, becomes a beam to pierce the thick skin and hard heart of the old Adam. He is a tireless self projector who would rather see the world go than himself contradicted. He can get personal theology and apersonal mysticism to serve his turn. But the *representation* of death contradicts him. It puts him in his penultimate place in the ordinary social world. It opens the possibility of a new humanity of communion with other selves. By relativizing self, it saves him from the worst that self can do. When the image of death has made us recognize the finitude of our own persons, we are at last free to recognize our neighbours and begin loving them as ourselves. We are saved into the relativities of communion by acknowledging our own relativity. The apersonality of God, touching our clenched selves so that they break open, starts off the properly human being who cares for others. Participation in the representation of Christ's death restores us to our common humanity.

Back at the altar again, we find it all represented in few words and sparse action. Christ, with death and the dissolution of his personality upon him, takes the only remaining initiative by giving what he still (just) is as person, to others for their good. He does it in a symbol, so that it can be seen whole and at once. The bread "is my body given for you". So the dreaded reality beyond persons can be grace and life when it comes to us mediated through the right hands, in the right symbol. And we come back to the altar again and again to assimilate, not just it, but the way it is done too — because our neighbours need us to know by second nature how to do it for them.

Afterthought about Representations

In thinking about representations — pictorial, dramatic, ritual and theological — we have sometimes been distrustful and suspicious, sometimes trusting and appreciative. But all the time, we knew that we were dealing with representations. This was not an artificial exercise. It is not just when we are reading or otherwise taking time to size things up critically that we deal with representations. We do it all the time.

The knowledge we get about God, ourselves and other people is never static. We are always pushing it on into the realm of what we do not know yet by means of guesses and beliefs. These guesses come out of what we know by experience, but they are representations and not things themselves. If they work, they carry us to things which we have not known before and help us to understand them. Their goal and reward is truth. They themselves are fictions.

They share in truth by coming from truth and getting to truth. To get over the bar, the pole-vaulter has to imagine himself getting over it before he does so. He makes a fiction in his mind for his body to follow. Representations are necessary to get from one place to another. They go, and take us, from actuality to actuality. If it were not for them, actuality would be just one damn thing after another with no meaning, human or divine. They hold our lives together by giving them meaning. We guess by coaxing the meaning out of what we have already experienced, shaping it to aim it at what we do not yet know and what has not yet happened.

We need to distinguish between representations and actualities for quite practical reasons. Because doing anything involves a running together, even a necessary confusion, of the two, by which we trick ourselves, we need help from somebody else who observes from outside. The pole-vaulter watches a slow-motion video tape of his performance with his trainer. If it went wrong, the trainer will tell the athlete that he made the fault because he was imagining wrongly and suggest ways of imagining which will work better. A religious person who is trying to live his religion will consult a sensible clergyman in order to revise his imaginary aims in life in the light of what is possible. Inadequate religious imagination, whether too grand or too weak, causes inadequate religious living. If we do not make these distinctions, our imagination does not work for us. We may well imagine strongly and impressively, but the practical effect will be futile or damaging.

This can be applied to our preoccupation with the Christian eucharist. People who believed that the bread and wine are not symbolic but are changed into actual flesh and blood by the spell of consecration, have treated it in thoroughly inappropriate ways. They could sometimes be so overwhelmed by the error that they withdrew from full participation in the sacrament. They could sometimes be so pleased with it that they fed the sacrament to their domestic animals in order to fatten them. Reacting against such negative and positive abuses, Protestant reformers made strong assertions of the symbolic character of the bread and wine and of the distance in time between the rite and the death of Jesus which it commemorated. Distinct from Christ's body, blood and death, the bread and wine mediated to people the meaning of them. They had a point. The eucharist is a threshold, a moment betwixt-and-between Christ's past, actual and physical life and death, and the actual and physical lives and future deaths faced by the participants. It is a present moment which, like all present moments, is a mathematical line without thickness between what has happened and what is to come. So it is well marked by the transparency of symbol. It is futile to take the eucharist purely literally, fertile to take it symbolically as representation of what was actual and is to become actual again. For the eucharistic congregation to say "We are the people of God" is nothing but vain complacency if literally meant. If it is meant in gratitude and hope it is a spur to the actual moral performances, the good works, which can alone make it actually true, and really present, to the man in the street — a keen and critical observer of moral performances.

The same rules apply to religious doctrines, which are also representations. If we take them *au pied de la lettre* we either assent to them or dissent from them. We either say "That's that" or "That's not it", and are not any the better or wiser for saying either. Everyone knows that adherents of religious doctrines are not, by virtue of their adherence, better or wiser than other people. Sometimes they are sillier and worse. The same applies to those who reject the doctrines. Both miss their meanings by ignoring their symbolic character. They would stand to get it if they browsed more. A doctrine should be contemplated with the mind and heart as a picture is. It has to be savoured, played with, patiently and acutely analysed, if it is to yield the food of its meaning. Then it will have a social future, a useful life among people.

7

Life-Giving Criticism

In the preceding chapter we noticed the importance of distinguishing between actualities and representations of them. The Protestant reformers were keen on this difference in the context of the eucharist. The actual death of Christ, his actual blood and body, were not the same as the liturgical representation of them. In passing we glimpsed something else, which is the opposite of this but not less important. It was the "necessary confusion" of representation and actuality by means of which we temporarily trick ourselves in the interests of getting things done. "The object of religion is conduct," said Matthew Arnold; "and if a man helps himself in his conduct by taking an object of hope and presentiment as if it were an object of certainty, he may be said thereby to gain an advantage." (*Literature and Dogma*, Chapter IV, first paragraph.) We run imagination and actuality together as a way of getting places and doing things. In this chapter we will try to get a better balance and interaction between this running together and this taking apart. Taking a rest from our preoccupation with the eucharist — but with no promises that it may not crop up at some point — we will make the other common christian exercise of Bible reading the field for this attempt.

Christianity has a body of scripture which is sacred. It is handed on as a major ingredient of its identity. Yet it has allowed it to be subjected to minute and relentless criticism, often based on spectacularly secular ideas about how texts are made and understood. This looks like a classic instance of an irresistible force meeting an unmoveable object. The Bible is fixed, regular and canonical. But its readers include eccentric as well as orthodox people, those who like stability and those who prefer change. Bishops and priests are meant to guard the Bible. Critics attack it. The two roles have been combined. There have been cardinals of the Roman Catholic Church who have also been biblical critics. The Church of England has usually had a biblical critic or two on the bench of bishops, even archbishops such as William Temple and Michael Ramsey. Such people make it look as if cherishing the Bible and criticizing it is not a flat contradiction or a hopeless muddle of intentions. I am a priest and a critic. I celebrate the Holy Communion service and I criticize the Bible. At the Holy Communion I break the bread, which represents Christ, and then serve it to whoever is there as their spiritual food. At my desk I break the gospels, which again represent Christ, in ways which are meant to make them, too, digestible. In both, something holy and whole is taken apart. That is how it is made available to other people as food for the mind or soul. The holiness is not annihilated but digested. Holy bread and holy texts are transformed into holy living. The truth is our bread.

Like most Christian things, having canonical holy texts and criticizing them goes back to the Jews. So let us watch two rabbis. Before doing so we need to know that when one of them talks about "the secrets of the chariot" he means the symbolically fraught and mind-blowing revelation of God's chariot-throne in the first chapters of Ezekiel. This text (referred to earlier for the surrealism and ambivalence of its imaging of God) was famous among the rabbis for its ability to ignite mystical states in minds which dwelt on it. Here is the story. It comes from the great treasury of Rabbinic biblical exegesis *Midrash Rabbah* (1:10:2)

> Once as Rabbi Ben Azzai sat and expounded [the scriptures], the fire played around him. They went and told Rabbi Akiba saying "Sir, as Rabbi Ben Azzai sits and expounds, the fire is flashing round him." He [Akiba] went to him and said to him "I hear that as you were expounding, the fire flashed round you ... Were you perhaps treating of the secrets of the chariot?" "No" replied Rabbi Ben Azzai, "No, I was only linking up the words of the Law of Moses with one another and then with the words of the prophets, and the prophets with the psalms and wisdom writings, and the words rejoiced as when they were delivered from Mount Sinai, and they were sweet as at their original utterance."

Good criticism, criticism around which creative fire sparkles, stands on the same level with the great and holy writings themselves. It is in communion with them. Critical precision and vivacity do for a writing what that writing did for the reality it addressed. They make its presence real and let it live, the words rejoicing in their original, fresh sweetness. The holy fire of creativity plays around the conjunction of text and critic, kindled by a devout skill which is like prayer, because criticism too is a reticent expectancy.

But just what sort of criticism was Rabbi Ben Azzai doing? First, the story makes the point that it was workaday, routine stuff. He was not explaining "the secrets of the chariot", the volatile and almost automatically inflammable record of Ezekiel's vision. It was the bread and butter of law — law above all — and prophets and writings. Ben

Azzai's technique was "linking up". He connected. He even confused. Like a host, he introduced texts to texts which had not met before, or, if they had, not quite like this. And the individuality of each was refreshed by the conjunction. These linkings must, necessarily, conceal and presuppose partings. A host invites people to leave their homes so as to enjoy themselves, and give enjoyment to others, at his place. Rabbi Ben Azzai's invitations were sent out all over the biblical texts, among laws and prophets and prayers and proverbs. His skill in making an apt guest list, full of happy possibilities of conjunction, resulted in a good time, with all lit up. As their reward for uprooting themselves from their own places, they were refreshed by the happiness of rediscovering themselves in new contexts and conjunctions.

There is another way. Instead of getting people to come to his place, the critic can visit them in their own homes, becoming a visitor rather than a host. This was the aim of another Bible reader in a different culture from Ben Azzai's.

The great English philosopher John Locke spent his august old age as a permanent and honoured guest in an Essex country house. He enjoyed welcome stability and space there at the end of a life in which he had suffered uprooting and exile for his political allegiance. As he had long meant to do, he turned his attention to the Bible. He wrote an excellent and influential book about Jesus called *The Reasonableness of Christianity as Delivered in the Scriptures*. It was published in 1695. Its title admits us to a world very different from Ben Azzai's, cooler and less prone to fire hazards. The scriptures under criticism are the gospels, and Locke read them with that sense of historical distance which the rabbis used only occasionally if it helped them with more pressingly present concerns. Locke tried to make it his constant guide. He realized that Jesus had had his own place and time, along with his own concerns, and that these inform the gospels. This made them books from a once-living past, and not just handbooks or theological quarries for seventeenth-century preachers. Locke did not expect the gospels to contain the full apparatus of the orthodox Christian doctrine of his own day. His suspicion of dogma in any form averted him from that. Instead he found a Jesus who adjusted his teaching, which was in any case more ethical than dogmatic, to the political pressures of first-century Judea under Roman occupation. The one essential doctrine in the gospels was that Jesus is the Messiah. But Jesus, as attentive gospel readers often notice with surprise, was reticent about it and very wary of letting it out. His motive was accommodation to political reality: "to keep the heady and hasty multitude from such Disorder, as would have involved him in it; and have disturbed the course and cut short the time of his Ministry". The doctrine needed careful timing. So it was best kept obscure until its hour came. This was after Jesus' resurrection "when there should be no longer any fear that it should cause any disturbance in Civil Societies and the Governments of the World. But he could not [during his ministry] declare himself to be the Messiah without manifest danger of Tumult and Sedition." At that particular time, the truth about him was "for those who were well-disposed now [not political fanatics], or would reflect on it when the whole course of his ministry was over".

Locke went to the gospels as a friendly and understanding foreign visitor to a country not his own. He read them as a homogeneous set, and without much interest in the individuality of each. He took bits from them — an impressively large enough collection of bits to support his case about Jesus – in order to reconstruct their past, which was different from his Christian present. Like Ben Azzai he linked verses to verses, but he wanted to recover Jesus in his first-century situation. He was more history-minded. Yet, whether he was entirely aware of it or not, his own times were also in his mind, guiding, perhaps sometimes unconsciously, his choices of material. He had experienced the tumult and sedition made by overheated dogma, political and religious. He had been a refugee. Now he wanted the peace which he at last enjoyed in Essex to be the normal life of an England settled in the peace of a tolerant society. Tolerance demanded the restraint of doctrinal passions, even when the doctrine was true, for the sake of the great blessing of peace. So his interest in the first century was shaped by his interest in his own seventeenth century. He meant his historical work to do it some good. That good was more like a cooling breeze, allaying fevers, than Ben Azzai's magic fire. Historical distance helped to get things cool and clear. His work too brought sweetness and freshness to ancient texts by linking verse to verse in a sustaining wholeness. But the wholeness which he made was in the past. Letting the past speak for itself was the best treatment for the ills of the present.

It was the sort of work that required prolonged reading of the sacred texts in the quiet of his study. To recover the whole reality in the gospels he needed to give the gospels more time than they get in church, where a bit of them is read and soon swallowed into a sermon, becoming grist for the preacher's mill. He found this even more important with St Paul's letters, to which he turned next. He wanted to do justice to St Paul, to understand him charitably and sympathetically. This meant hearing him out, reading whole letters and not depending on the fragments he got in church. Then he saw that Paul, though often criticized – in an idle form of criticism – as impossibly obscure, had comprehensible arguments. But they were arguments about problems besetting him and his churches around the Mediterranean in the first century. They were not the same as the arguments which bothered Locke's contemporaries. Were the Gentiles as freely admissible to the Christian community as Jews? Should some strings of Jewish tradition be attached to their entry? This was a major crisis for Paul, requiring a rethinking of the whole meaning of biblical history, starting with Adam. It was one of the few problems about Christianity which seventeenth-century Anglicans did *not* have – because, thanks to Paul's intransigent and strenuous efforts, it had been settled as he had wanted it to be. The Gentiles were in for good and all (and the problem for a seventeenth-century reader like Locke was the opposite and historical one of how the Jews had ever fitted in to the origins of Christianity at all). So as well as reading Paul's letters right through, the modern reader needed to read, as it were between their lines, the particular and past situation which they addressed: Jewish Christianity secure and established, Gentile Christianity an open question as awkward as the open question of women priests in our own day. Locke exercised charity by sympathetically standing alongside Paul as he coped with his problems; just as any Christian is obliged, by the commandment to love his neighbour, to exercise charity by standing alongside any struggling fellow human-being. Locke exercised justice by seeing Paul in the context of the pressures upon him and by giving him his full say, just as any good judge has to do with any plaintiff.

It was a way of reading the scriptures critically which appealed to much of the best in people – not only to important principles of fairness and sympathy, but to the practical use of those principles and those scriptures within the lively context of our interest in other people's lives.

This made an enormous difference to the way Christians, from Locke's time onwards, read the Old Testament. They could no longer be content with the old way of reading the ancient Jewish scriptures as a rag-bag of prophecies of Christianity. This imperialistic attitude had to yield to the realization that the prophets and scribes of the Old Testament were people like Paul with their own insights and feelings in response to their own problems and achievements. It was here that Christians, of the generation after Locke, began to realize that the justice and charity required by critical reading were graces which were not cheap, could even cost them some of their oldest and dearest securities, their oldest colonies. They had to do justice to the Jews.

For example: St Matthew says in his gospel (1:22-3) that Jesus' conception by the Holy Spirit, rather than a natural father, "was done, that it might be fulfilled which was spoken of the Lord by the prophet, saying, Behold, a virgin shall be with child, and shall bring forth a son, and they shall call his name Emmanuel, which being interpreted is, God with us." When St Matthew wrote this he was doing as Rabbi Ben Azzai did. He linked words from the prophets, Isaiah 7:14 in this case, into his story of Jesus' birth. It gave the old words themselves a new birth. The story, as St Matthew told it, was very like the old story of the childhood of Moses, the great man of the law. Like Moses, Jesus escaped a massacre of male children. Like Moses, Jesus came out of Egypt. Matthew was linking his verses of old scripture together to establish Christianity in its native matrix of sacred Jewish history. He and his fellow Christians certainly believed that this revived the old words with the freshness of new actuality "sweet as at their original utterance". It was their homecoming, their fulfilment. But a reading along Locke's history-minded lines does not stop there. It goes back to the original context of Isaiah's words, to the hole in Isaiah's book which has been made by Matthew lifting these words from it. It reads the entire seventh chapter of Isaiah and not just its fourteenth verse, and recovers a rich and gripping historical context which St Matthew left behind as irrelevant. Around 735 BC, Syria and Israel were in league against Judah. The King of Judah was alarmed, but God sent Isaiah to him to tell him not to be. The hostile league would not last. God would give him a vivid guarantee of it. A young woman would conceive and bear a son, calling him Emmanuel. Before this child had reached years of discretion, Syria and Israel would be devastated and powerless.

For anyone like Locke who gives priority to the original setting of words, the setting of the Emmanuel prophecy in Isaiah's book will have priority over its setting in Matthew's book. Then the tables will have been turned. The Hebrew prophet has been done justice. Is anyone going to speak up for the Christian evangelist? And if so, how?

Locke had a radical young friend called Anthony Collins who was notorious as a free-thinker. Collins collected books. Among them was an account in a French magazine of how Jewish rabbis interpret the scripture, how they link verse to verse by virtue of their purely literary features, apart from their historical contexts. Matthew had linked Isaiah's young woman to Jesus' virgin mother because in the Greek translation of the Hebrew bible – which Matthew and the early Christians generally used – the word used for Isaiah's young woman was "parthenos", which meant "virgin". It struck Collins that an evangelist like Matthew was a close cousin to the rabbis, indeed closer to them than to seventeenth-century Anglicans. Matthew was working by rabbinic rules, and by those rules his use of Isaiah is justified. The rabbis were always doing that sort of thing. The unrabbinic seventeenth-century reader did not. But he, said Collins, could understand it as allegorical. Allegory is a way of delivering an event or an image from the bounds of its original, concrete and particular setting for use somewhere else. It is very common in religions at large. Isaiah had already used allegory when he made an ordinary child into a sign of the political future. He did it by way of the child's name, Emmanuel: names being more allegorical than the children themselves and this name being tailored to the message. So Isaiah made the child an allegory with significance beyond himself. And Matthew is doing nothing out of the way in projecting the allegorizing process which Isaiah began into a further, early Christian, stage. As Collins shrewdly observed, new religions do not like to look new. Allegory was a way of linking them to the old sacred tradition.

The book in which Collins said this, *A Discourse of the Grounds and Reasons of the Christian Religion*, came out in 1724 and caused a furore of the sort that *Honest to God* and *The Myth of God Incarnate* have made recently – the sort of furore that innovative critical works always make. Unlike Locke, Collins was a troublemaker and, unlike Locke again, much more interested in making a stir than in promoting Christianity. But if the Bible and Church history are anything to go by, troublers of tradition are as much part of the living religious process as its guardians. And Collins was right about history. In particular, he was historically right to connect early Christian biblical interpretation with rabbinic interpretation. In general, he was right to see religion as a growing thing which develops by getting new meanings out of old words.

Or is it? Collins made trouble because the great majority of churchgoers did not want to see their religion, particularly their Holy Bible, as he had described it. He said it changed and they believed it to be unchanging. He made a division which they did not want by setting the gospels firmly in a past where things like reading the Bible were done in ways which looked very strange to people like himself. He made a connection they did not want by showing an evangelist working like a rabbi. He was, in fact, raising basic questions which still perplex and disturb religious people, bubbling to the surface of Church life whenever anything new, like ordaining women to the priesthood or altering liturgies, comes on the scene. Is Christianity the same yesterday, today and forever, or does it change? Is Christianity something simple and single, or is it plural and diverse with Paul doing it one way, Matthew another, and we in yet more versions? In the end, our understanding of God is tied up with these questions and our answers. So we need to take them slowly and carefully, getting the feel of them at the sort of depth which religious questions have and hoping to get clues towards answers at that depth too.

8

Jesus: Self Becomes Social

Depth in human life is tied up with memory, with remembering. Individually, we feel that our lives have depth by being rich in memories. Children hoard them eagerly and the old, for whom other kinds of riches have come and gone, live largely on them. They are not only in the mind. The cluttered mantelpiece and the stuffed album and address book hold them too. A smell, a taste, a flower or a visit to old haunts can release them with the over-whelming force of depths suddenly flooding up over our superficialities, of time suddenly felt so profoundly that it seems, paradoxically, to have stopped or missed a beat. Psychologists believe, and have found that the belief works, that when there is something so deeply wrong with our feelings that we cannot function properly, the root of the trouble lies in memories deeper than consciousness. The way to the remedy is Memory Lane. The remedy itself is the remembering of what we had forgotten because we could not fit it in – until now, when our remembering sessions have reconstructed a past rich and strongly linked enough to bear it at last.

We do not call our personal memories "tradition". "Tradition" stands for corporate memory, the store of remembrance which gives depth to the life of a social group – by which, like any individual, a group understands itself. The Church is such a group, outstanding in the vast wealth of memories which make up its tradition. Here too the memories are not only in the mind. In ordinary usage "church" does not mean a group of people, still less a concept. It is a building you go to. And as soon as you enter it you see a clutter of objectified memories on a much grander scale than our personal mementos and souvenirs. Walking through the churchyard you were besought by tombstones to remember people you never even knew, whom nobody still around can have known. Individual memory, memory of individuals, does not last as long as their choice of stone and words suggests that they thought it would. But once inside the church you see the corporate mementos, the texts, the images in glass and paint and sculpture, the records of benefactions to the poor of the parish, the font and the altar. The perspective is long, going right back to mythical Adam. The scope includes moments of death and grief, of return and happiness. If a service is going on, there will also be memories in words and movements. We all have our own memories, but here is something longer and bigger, the deep, unfathomable well of a remote past which opens on to the present.

It all looks so much more permanent and stable than we feel — or than the churchyard made us feel — about our lives. These things stay. They are the things of God: "O, Thou who changest not, abide with me." Yet we know, and the things themselves confess it, that they came here in and through time. A painted board says that Thomas Mudd gave ten pounds to buy bread for the poor in 1723. This stained glass window recalls the crucifixion, but also Emily Watson who died in 1872. This Bible was printed in 1970 and contains translations of texts which can also be dated, if less precisely. So we take notice that these things have a history. We may imagine that history to have been as stately and assured as this church – a sort of liturgical procession. But closer inspection reveals something riskier and less august along with the dignity. We could read some Church history and recover some of the ungainly struggles and uncertainties out of which our stately and venerable creeds were made. Or, taking less time, we might follow the service of Holy Communion, the Church's arch-memory with its strongly physical presence, the memory round which all the other mementos in the church and the churchyard cluster.

It is a service that gathers and turns around memory: the memory of the night on which Jesus was betrayed. He and his disciples, round their table, went through the dignified and homely Passover ritual. Within its recollected ceremony there was recollection of the fraught night long ago when their Jewish forebears snatched a quick meal in preparation for unsettlement and risky escape. And this particular Passover was, too, agitated by something more than routine. Like the first one, it took place at the edge of flight and uprooting, on "the night in which he was betrayed". This dread became more than a sinister penumbra. It was fastened into the symbolic centre of the ritual when Jesus made the bread represent his own doomed body, betrayed and to be broken.

Here, facing death and dissolution, was a man with his own memories of God: God in his own life through the tradition, the accumulation of common Jewish memory, which had fed and formed him, which he was drawing on now. It all comes together in him, in his individual, and suddenly very lonely, body. He links it all to that. The body is all he, like the rest of us, has. And it is fragile and mortal. What will become of it, of him? The answer is in what he does with the bread. In a definitive symbol and a brave stroke of allegory he calls it his body. He breaks it. He gives it to the people around him. So it is saved and given a future: first by being represented in the bread, then by being broken, then by being given away to others. First he takes the bread of ancient tradition. It is what we all do when we take up a religious tradition and make it our own as a representation of our own lives. This is how we live and learn, not only in religion. Then he breaks it. It is the moment when what is whole and cherished, what has taken so long and so much care in its own coming to be, and then its coming to be ours, cracks apart. This too is part of our living and learning. Even religion, which binds and integrates life in apparently strong and stable tradition, comes apart at the seams under the wear and tear of time. Bodies of knowledge and tradition are not so different from physical bodies. Corporate "selves" have to go through the same ordeal as individual selves.

But this is not the end. Breaking is part of the process of living, as we have seen in the example of biblical criticism. It is a necessary preliminary to giving. So the people round the table, when they took the bread, took a tradition which their master had linked to his individual body, then broken so that it could get into their bodies. They are being gathered into the stream of life in which individual cells draw on nourishment, become themselves, and then become the nourishment of others – the stream of life of which death is a creative and necessary part: one body's end becoming other bodies' beginning. In the context of religious tradition its opposite is the hopeless attempt to keep symbolic tradition in intensive care for ever. That attitude conceals a belief that the death of tradition would be utter and final loss and could not possibly be a gift to others. Its fear of loss makes it afraid of life, and even, perhaps, in the long run, atheist in a confused and shame-faced way.

There is a lot at stake here. So rather than continuing in polemic, let us return to the New Testament and use a critical sense of it as a way of appropriating part of the lively process of history. There are other, and major, examples there of the pattern we have observed at the table. We will look for the patterns of movement which, in scripture as elsewhere, give words their power. The patterns, the dynamic structures, are as deep down as we can get into the sources of life.

Paul's letters testify, passionately, to his belief in the death of Christ as the source of new religious life. They are forceful because this is a belief which Paul does not place in something right outside himself, but knows as the turning point of his own biography. He presses it on others as a transforming gift because he has absorbed it into himself. Hence, in an odd mixture of humility and pushiness, he presses himself on others – yet not himself, he says, but the Christ in him; and not to overwhelm those others, he says, but to nourish their growth by getting them to die to their old or current selves and live for others. He seeks to convert them because he has been converted. What was that conversion? It was what religious people most dread, the death of their tradition. Paul used the word "law" as the inclusive label for that tradition. This was because he had been a pharisaic Jew, focusing the whole of his religious inheritance on obedience to scripture as law. The death of Christ, he said, was simultaneously the death of the law. Whatever else that means, it shows that his own religious life underwent a catastrophe which was equivalent to Christ's death and affected by it. His religion, which was all that he had and integrated all that he had, came apart.

It was a loss like death. Yet when we read his letters *it is all still there*. They are crowded and vivid with the scriptures he had studied devoutly before. Adam, Abraham and Moses are never out of his thoughts. They are alive to him. He not only quotes scripture copiously. Its ideas and patterns survive in him. The way of moral obedience is still the way he walks. He still thinks by thinking about scripture. What had happened? He had found a new centre around which all the contents of his mind and heart, all the tradition he had absorbed, lived new life. Where "law" had been the inclusive centre, now it is Christ: Christ's body. He understood the transition as the beginning of life, as resurrection beyond death. He had rediscovered God. He had lost everything and got it all back.

Paul shows us the vital pattern in his pass-over movement between his Jewish tradition and his Christianity. The gospels have interested studious people, since Locke at least, for what they tell us about the transition from Jesus to Christianity. This is a clinically historical way of reading them. It gets its emotional and religious power from its hope of discovering what Jesus was really like (e.g. for Locke, an undogmatic and prudent Messiah with an ethical message). But it soon notices that the gospels, its only resource in this fascinating quest, have lives of their own. Locke only glimpsed the possibility of this when he noticed that they sometimes disagreed with one another. But he did not make much of it, or notice that it might be a sign that each of the evangelists had a life and gospel of his own. Collins made the gospel writers, particularly Matthew, more vivid. They were a kind of Christian rabbis, busily handling scriptural prophecies according to the outlandish norms of the time and religion's perpetual delight in allegory. It was a correct picture, though as unwelcome to the modern devout as it was startling to all but the most robust scholars. In our own century, the liveliness of the gospels, as something more than aseptic or characterless records of Jesus, has come to be appreciated in two stages.

What is called (it is a misleadingly dull label) form criticism was an awakening to the truth that the life of Christ's successors, the first two generations of Christians, was as much part of the gospels as Christ's own life. These were books for contemporary people and churches. They were meant to be useful, not just interesting. They drew on oral traditions about Jesus, memories of him which were valued for their practical religious value and not as archival material. And what the first Christians valued, they made much of, exploited and used. A parable in chapter 25 of St Matthew's gospel tells of a lord who left good sums of money with his servants before leaving them. When he came back he expected them to have been used and increased. He was hard on the man who had carefully wrapped up his money and buried it (to change the metaphor, put it in intensive care). It is a sign of the success of early Christianity that it used and augmented what Jesus had left it. It does make things hard for the historical researcher, however, who would like to find sayings of Jesus in mint condition, not worn or encrusted by their intensive practical use, who would like to find at least one bit of Jesus' legacy wrapped in a napkin and buried. It was not that the form-critics thought that there was little or nothing of what Jesus had said or done in the gospels. It was that everything of Jesus in the gospels had been appropriated, used and digested, long before the researchers could get at it, by sprightly and practically creative Christians. So for lack of an agreed centre to start from, form criticism ran out in multiple options and reconstructions. But its exponents deserve sympathy and praise. They were scholars who looked beyond their own lives of order and precision into the fertile tangles of real religious life. They were modern Christians who wanted to find Christ for themselves, yet did their best to do justice to the people who got in the way of their search, those first-century Christians who had consumed and augmented Jesus' legacy instead of freezing it. They tried to do justice to Jesus' own feeding of his own life into the lives of his followers; to that profound usefulness of what Jesus said and did which made it a practical and adaptable heritage rather than a venerated antique.

But still, there were historical facts. For one, it was quite clear that Jesus was an oral teacher. Even teachers who, unlike Jesus, write their own books, know that as soon as they publish them they lose control of them. They can be understood and misunderstood as anybody sees fit. Indignant protests by hurt authors in the correspondence columns of the literary weeklies against unfair treatment by reviewers never really mend matters. With oral teachers it all happens instantly and irrevocably. As a result, we can never be sure, in the gospels, that we have what Jesus said unmixed with what other people made of it. Precisely because his words cut deep and their justice and charity kindled the imagination and moral purpose of those who heard them, they, his hearers and interpreters, are there in the gospels too.

A couple of analogies should make clear that this is part of being alive and not just an inconvenience. It sometimes seems that critics are looking for Jesus' own words as if they hoped that they would be like the seeds they buy in garden shops, hermetically sealed in little foil packets inside paper ones. But it is not like that. All that they can get to is the garden or hedgerow in which the seeds have germinated and flourished within their surrounding ecologies. They have become plants which have themselves seeded and generated other plants. Or think of a commonplace oral event, a minor row between friends. Exactly what anyone said and meant by it immediately becomes a part of the dispute, in which certainty is not to be disentangled from quick adaptations of it one way or another. It is precisely because it mattered so much, wound people up and set them off, that it is impossible to get it back in its pristine state.

There is another historical fact, or set of them. Although we do not possess the words of Jesus in aseptically sterile form like the seeds in the packet, we do have plants which germinated from them. We have the gospels, preserved in writing. We also have the historical fact that one gospel seeded another. We are not sure of the order. The current consensus is that Mark's gospel, seeded by oral tradition, itself seeded Matthew's and Luke's where we find their altered versions of what Mark wrote. But it may be that Matthew or Luke wrote before Mark. We do not know. What we do know is that the evangelists were creative exploiters of their materials. And we do possess the texts which each of them wrote in the final versions which got into the Christian canon of scripture. It needs to be said that even this is relative. Because the gospel texts were copied by hand and by people with views of their own about what they should say, they are full of little disputable differences between the surviving written texts. But from the third century, when Christianity had to get its act together as the uniform religion of the Roman empire, the pressures to be conservative of the details of the texts was strong. They had become holy. They were frozen, and interpretation of them, which flourished more than ever, was to be done in separate commentaries rather than, in the manner of the evangelists themselves, mulched into the texts. So each gospel is a dependable enough record of what its author thought and felt.

Work on the gospels in the last fifty years has achieved portraits of the evangelists which are vivid, detailed and rounded. We now know Mark as a fierce and secretive writer. He was pessimistic about human nature. Even Jesus' closest disciples are far from understanding him and in the end, desert him. The salvation which he brings to humanity has a mysterious and alien quality which means that it works by sudden strikes. It tears the fabric of the world like a new patch on a threadbare old coat, like the ferment of new wine bursting old and hardened leather bottles (Mark 2:22). He teaches in provocative riddles which break up conventional thinking if you see them, bounce off it if you do not. He is an unsettled wanderer who usually thinks on his feet. Matthew has him sit in authoritative stability and majesty to give his great Sermon on the Mount. And the teaching he gives is more direct and plain than in Mark. His disciples understand it, though they have little of the faith needed to enact it. It does not so much burst the conventional containers as fill them to overflowing with an excess of powerful new meaning. Salvation is available in the strict but supportive frame of the Christian community, and it is got by the performance of moral duties which are demanding but possible – whereas for Mark the whole duty of the disciple was to follow Jesus to death. Luke's Jesus is an altogether friendlier person. His ethics are universal philanthropy – the theme to which he boils down Matthew's much longer Sermon on the Mount. He is to be found at dinner parties, letting other people have their say and developing it. He is optimistic about human nature. Even people who have gone far astray, like Zacchaeus the tax-farmer or the prodigal son or the unjust steward, can be saved if they look life in the face shrewdly and with realistic optimism. His disciples are fallible but ultimately dependable. Mark left the great Peter in tears of remorse at his denial of Jesus, and had no more to say of him. In Luke Jesus himself promises Peter that he will overcome his failure and become the leader and supporter of his brethren.

These thumbnail sketches are meant to bring out the distinct individuality of each evangelist. But they were also a group who sparked one another off and controlled one another. Mark's sense of the gospel as disruptive and unworldly was not denied by Matthew. Rather he kept it as a warning to the slack and the hypocritical that, though they might get by in the world, at the great court session of doomsday they would be punished. For Luke, Jesus was a prophet sent by God to disrupt the easy confidence of the Jews in their privileged status as God's people. Their failure to attend to his inspired warnings because they were an unwelcome interruption, was fatal for their future. So Mark's strong discontinuity is not ignored by his successors but geared in to the fabric of more workaday and natural religious life to rouse it and energize it.

Biblical criticism and the bread of the eucharist have combined to teach us a lesson about what Christianity has to offer us. It is initiation into the pattern by which what is old can become new, what is bound to die can be distributed into life in new forms. In the middle of it is the dangerous but indispensable moment when the text or the bread is grasped in order to be taken apart. It is a moment of loss and leavetaking of the sort which we know from our own lives to be critically difficult. It does not necessarily come out well. Crises can break us and make us nasty, or make us and make us good. We need to know how to handle them for the best — which is not just our own best, but the best for the people we live with too.

Is there "no such thing as society"? On the contrary, our individual selves are social to the core. Physically, every body is a temporary aggregation of cells. It survives so long as they get on well with one another in the complex relations of consuming and being consumed which go on inside us all the time. Psychologically and religiously, every soul is a temporary nexus of memories and pressures, hopes and fears, which keeps going for as long as they can feed and tolerate one another.

A rabbi had a dream. First he saw hell. People were seated round a table. In the middle was a bowl of food. Each person had a very long spoon, the end of it being fastened to his or her hand. They dug in to the food, then found that the spoons were so long that they could not get the food at the far end of them into their mouths. The result was a horrible scene of frustrated hunger and wasted nourishment. The people cursed one another as they spattered the food which they could not get into themselves. Then the scene changed. It was heaven. The arrangement was exactly the same: the table, the bowl of food in the middle, the long spoons tied to the people's hands. But now the people had discovered that, although no one could feed him or her self, every one could feed the person opposite. So the food got into the people, and instead of the cursing there was the happy murmur of people enjoying both the gratification of eating and the social sustenance, the interest and pleasure, of getting to know one another.

Is there no such thing as the self? On the contrary, society is made of selves to the core, and would not exist without them. A society is a temporary aggregation of selves. It keeps going so long as the selves get on well with one another, can cross over to one another, in the complex relations of consuming and being consumed which go on among us all the time. Society is hell when the motto is "eat or be eaten". Society is heaven when the motto is "eat and be eaten". The Christian eucharist is a representation of the conviviality which we should make our own by assimilation — which takes a life and a lifetime.

I Believe
Trevor Huddleston

A simple, prayerful series of reflections on the phrases of the Creed. This is a beautiful testament of the strong, quiet inner faith of a man best known for his active role in the Church – and in the world.

The Heart of the Christian Faith
Donald Coggan

The author ". . . presents the essential core of Christianity in a marvellously simple and readable form, quite uncluttered by any excess of theological technicality."

The Yorkshire Post

Be Still and Know
Michael Ramsey

The former Archbishop of Canterbury looks at prayer in the New Testament, at what the early mystics could teach us about it, and at some practical aspects of Christian praying.

Pilgrim's Progress
John Bunyan

"A masterpiece which generation after generation of ordinary men and women have taken to their hearts."

Hugh Ross Williamson

Fount Paperbacks

Fount is one of the leading paperback publishers of religious books and below are some of its recent titles.

- ☐ FRIENDSHIP WITH GOD David Hope £2.95
- ☐ THE DARK FACE OF REALITY Martin Israel £2.95
- ☐ LIVING WITH CONTRADICTION Esther de Waal £2.95
- ☐ FROM EAST TO WEST Brigid Marlin £3.95
- ☐ GUIDE TO THE HERE AND HEREAFTER
                    Lionel Blue/Jonathan Magonet £4.50
- ☐ CHRISTIAN ENGLAND (1 Vol) David Edwards £10.95
- ☐ MASTERING SADHANA Carlos Valles £3.95
- ☐ THE GREAT GOD ROBBERY George Carey £2.95
- ☐ CALLED TO ACTION Fran Beckett £2.95
- ☐ TENSIONS Harry Williams £2.50
- ☐ CONVERSION Malcolm Muggeridge £2.95
- ☐ INVISIBLE NETWORK Frank Wright £2.95
- ☐ THE DANCE OF LOVE Stephen Verney £3.95
- ☐ THANK YOU, PADRE Joan Clifford £2.50
- ☐ LIGHT AND LIFE Grazyna Sikorska £2.95
- ☐ CELEBRATION Margaret Spufford £2.95
- ☐ GOODNIGHT LORD Georgette Butcher £2.95
- ☐ GROWING OLDER Una Kroll £2.95

All Fount Paperbacks are available at your bookshop or newsagent, or they can be ordered by post from Fount Paperbacks, Cash Sales Department, G.P.O. Box 29, Douglas, Isle of Man. Please send purchase price plus 22p per book, maximum postage £3. Customers outside the UK send purchase price, plus 22p per book. Cheque, postal order or money order. No currency.

NAME (Block letters) _____

ADDRESS_____

_____

_____